TEENS ~ ACTIONS, CONSEQUENCES, REWARDS

Facilitator Reproducible
Activities for Groups
and Individuals

Ester R.A. Leutenberg

Carol Butler, MS Ed, RN, C

Illustrated by
Amy L. Brodsky, LISW-S

Duluth, Minnesota

101 W. 2nd St., Suite 203
Duluth, MN 55802

800-247-6789

books@wholeperson.com
www.wholeperson.com

Teens – Actions, Consequences, Rewards
Facilitator Reproducible Activities for Groups and Individuals

Copyright ©2015 by Ester R.A. Leutenberg and Carol Butler. All rights reserved. Except for short excerpts for review purposes and materials in the activities and handouts sections, no part of this book may be reproduced or transmitted in any form by any means, electronic or mechanical without permission in writing from the publisher. Activities and handouts are meant to be photocopied.

All efforts have been made to ensure accuracy of the information contained in this book as of the date published. The author(s) and the publisher expressly disclaim responsibility for any adverse effects arising from the use or application of the information contained herein.

Printed in the United States of America

10 9 8 7 6 5 4 3 2 1

Editorial Director: Carlene Sippola
Art Director: Joy Morgan Dey
Assistant Art Director: Mathew Pawlak

Library of Congress Control Number: 2015939017
ISBN: 978-157025-330-0

The Purpose
Teens ~ Actions, Consequences, Rewards

This workbook was written to encourage teens to stop and think before they act,
consider the consequences of their actions,
and to capitalize on the rewards of positive actions.

Teens may turn a deaf ear to warnings about consequences.
A sense of invincibility says, "It won't happen to me."
A drive for rewards often outweighs the possibility of harm.

Adding into the mix …
  Adolescent hormones
  Quest for excitement
  Adrenaline of anger
  Chemistry of romance
  Self-Esteem issues
and then …
  Forethought goes out the window.

What *will* encourage typical, often headstrong, teens to stop and think?
Self-directed thoughts, decisions, and actions that lead to real rewards?
The excitement of risks coupled with probable positive outcomes?

The activities will help teens to consider these goals before acting:
Make decisions based on probable outcomes versus immediate gratification.
Uncover hidden consequences and rewards.
Discover healthy vs. unhealthy risks.
Define safe-risks.
Avoid preventable dangers.
Recognize positive attributes.
Handle difficult circumstances.
Work toward authentic rewards.

The value of this workbook:
Instead of being talked at – teens talk to each other.
Instead of being told to listen – teens listen to each other.
Instead of being pressured for perfection – teens express creatively.
Instead of being compelled to share – teens self-disclose at their discretion.
Instead of being told what to think – teens draw their own conclusions.
Instead of being passive – teens involve themselves in introspection and interaction.

**Teens are encouraged to think about consequences
and take risks … healthy and safe risks!**

Trust your heart if the seas catch fire, live by love though the stars walk backward.
~ E. E. Cummings

Format of the Book

Introduction for Teen Participants
　This introduction motivates the teens and helps them look forward to participating in the activities.
　Present the handout, page viii, as an overview before the first activity.

Cover page for each chapter
　Each chapter's cover page provides an inspirational quotation and describes each session to help facilitators accomplish the following:
- Select topics.
- Prepare the group.
- Stimulate discussion about the quotation.

　After the first activity in each chapter, teens may want to vote on which activity to do next.
　Unless otherwise stated, there is no particular order for the chapters or the handouts in the chapters.

Behavioral Coping Skills
　The back of each cover page lists the behavioral coping skills in each activity.
- Teens can preview the skills they will work on.
- Facilitators may use these as behavioral goals and competencies to evaluate.

Chapters
　FIRST ACTIVITY - *My Actions Book*
1. Healthy and Unhealthy Risks
2. Decisions
3. Types of Consequences and Rewards
4. Dangers
5. Attributes
6. Circumstances
7. Rewards

Recap of *Teens ~ Actions, Consequences, Rewards*

Versatility
- A chapter may serve as an entire workshop.
- Strategically select portions of the book to better match the skills you want to drive home.
- Facilitators may skip around by picking and choosing among different activities and chapters.
- Sessions may stand alone based on specific needs.
- Most handouts are adaptable to individual or group use.

Components in each session
　Reproducible handouts – Facilitators may photocopy and distribute sheets as they are presented, or they may white out and/or add text as desired and then photocopy.
　For the Facilitator – Information on the back of each handout:

  I. **Purpose**
　　The goals for the teens in each session.
  II. **Skills**
　　Behavioral objectives and competencies.
  III. **Possible Activities**
　　Ways to present topics and responses to elicit.
  IV. **Enrichment Activities**
　　Additional learning experiences; ways to conclude or follow up.

Introduction

Skills Teens will Practice in these Chapters

Chapter Cover Pages
　　Front: Skills defined for teens.
　　Back: Competencies listed for facilitators to evaluate.

Throughout this workbook, teens will be encouraged to engage in the following activities:
　　Demonstrate oral, written, and creative expression skills.
　　Practice giving and receiving feedback.

FIRST ACTIVITY - *My Actions Book*
- Organize work for safekeeping
- Identify the benefits of journals

Chapter 1. Healthy and Unhealthy Risks
- Self-assess risk factors
- Identify positive risks
- Plan safe actions
- Self-protect physically and emotionally
- Self-motivate

Chapter 2. Decisions
- Compare impulsive with thoughtful decisions
- Make and assess decisions
- Identify motives for actions
- Predict outcomes

Chapter 3. Types of Consequences and Rewards
- Identify types of consequences and rewards
- Compare genuine and superficial consequences and rewards
- Predict actions, consequences, and rewards

Chapter 4. Danger
- Personalize addiction and recovery concepts
- Identify recovery choices
- Describe violence prevention plans
- Connect food issues with emotions
- Promote safe driving.
- Discuss emotional aspects of sex
- Prevent self-harm
- Choose to live and thrive
- State gun safety concepts
- Prevent dating violence
- Break the bullying cycle
- Diminish gang involvement

Chapter 5. Attributes
- Practice healthy habits
- Develop positive traits
- Demonstrate transparency
- Promote positive change

6. Chapter Circumstances
- Replace dysfunction with function
- Recognize similarities despite differences
- Prevent avoidable problems
- Advocate for people in need
- Improve academic performance
- Decide when to fit in or opt out

7. Chapter Rewards
- Identify the rewards of hope
- Avoid or learn from mistakes
- Implement Mother Teresa's suggestions
- Acknowledge rewards of love and loss

Recap of *Teens ~ Actions, Consequences, Rewards*
- Self-assess comprehension of content
- Journal about current and future rewards
- State concepts learned in each chapter
- Complete *My Actions Book*

Ideas to Enhance Interest and Participation

> Before the first session, suggest that teens obtain a three-ring binder, a notebook or a scrapbook which will be the foundation of the **FIRST ACTIVITY -** *My Actions Book*.
>
> Have a three-ring hole punch and glue available. Encourage teens to save their completed handouts and related work. They can insert them in their *My Actions Book* as they complete them.
>
> The **FIRST ACTIVITY -** *My Actions Book*, page 13 and the concluding activity, **Recap –** *My Actions Book*, page 128 will explain how teens will preserve their work, personalize skills and maintain accomplishments.

Begin.
- Discuss the *Introduction for Teen Participants*, page vii, before the first activity.
- Read the quotation on the chapter cover page before the first activity in each chapter.

Prepare for each session.
- Review the page(s) and obtain materials – easily available paper, pens, markers, etc.
- Photocopy according to options selected – for individual or team formats, etc.

Create a comfortable climate.
- Assure teens: "What's on the completed handout stays on the handout and does not need to be shared."
- Promote confidentiality: "What's said in this room stays in this room."
- Remind teens to use code names, to avoid embarrassing anyone.
  - *Example: "MBS" for "My buddy Steve."*

Encourage positive risk-taking.
- Emphasize that positive actions yield rewards – the greater their involvement, the greater their growth. Suggest baby steps out of comfort zones – play a game, act in a skit, write a song, etc.

Empower teens.
- Explain that teens decide their levels of participation and disclosure; no one is pressured to share.
- Emphasize that perfect grammar, spelling, artistic talent, or ability to write or act are not required.

Emphasize rewards.
- Explain that not all actions lead to rewards. Some may lead to consequences.
- Remind teens that rewards are stronger motivators than punishments.

Make it fun to learn.
- The more teens talk and interact, the more teens learn.
- The more modalities the better; encourage expression through words, movement, music, art, etc.

Promote positive peer power.
- Teens watch and listen to peers more than they pay attention to adults.
- Encourage peer feedback, respectful debates, open minds, lively discussions, teamwork, etc.

Remember *Recap*, pages 121 to 128, when all of your selected sessions are completed.

Refer teens who seem to be experiencing difficulties to a school counselor, mental health or medical professional. If danger is imminent, call 911 or your local emergency services number, or arrange for teens to go to the nearest hospital emergency department.

Teens ~ Actions, Consequences, Rewards
Introduction for Teen Participants

RIDDLES
What do an astronaut and an actor have in common?
They could crash in outer space or at the box office. • They both take risks.
They could land on Mars or become movie stars. • They both want to reach for the stars.
They take calculated risks. • They have lots of people supporting them in their work.

What does a drunk driver and a person texting while walking on a pier have in common?
Poor judgment. • Not using common sense. • They think nothing bad happens.
They think they can luck out one more time. • They take risks without considering outcomes.

The older you get the more freedom you have to
To think for yourself.
To decide on your actions.
To work toward rewards.

Would you rather
Gamble on your life?
Or …take positive risks?

You choose!

The activities in this book will help guide you in these directions:

Explore your healthy and unhealthy risks.
Make decisions based on your predicted outcomes.
Uncover your hidden consequences and rewards.
Avoid preventable dangers.
Enhance your positive traits.
Handle your circumstances
Discover your rewards.

Trust your heart if the seas catch fire,
live by love though the stars walk backward.
~ E. E. Cummings

But remember …
Safety First!!!

If you or someone you know wants to harm self or others,
tell a trusted adult and/or call 911 or your local emergency services number,
or go to the nearest hospital emergency department.

Teens ~ Actions, Consequences, Rewards
TABLE OF CONTENTS

FIRST ACTIVITY *My Actions Book* 11
FIRST ACTIVITY *My Actions Book* **Behavioral Coping Skills** 12
    My Actions Book 13
        My Actions Book for the Facilitator 14

1. **Healthy and Unhealthy Risks** 15
    Healthy and Unhealthy Risks Behavioral Coping Skills 16
        Rate Your Risk Factors 17
            Rate Your Risk Factors for the Facilitator 18
        Risky the Robot 19
            Risky the Robot for the Facilitator 20
        My Early Warning System 21
            My Early Warning System for the Facilitator 22
        Positive Risks 23
            Positive Risks for the Facilitator 24
        Mind-Set: Sink or Swim 25
            Mind-Set: Sink or Swim for the Facilitator 26

2. **Decisions** 27
    Decisions Behavioral Coping Skils 28
        Stop and Think 29
            Stop and Think for the Facilitator 30
        My Decision Journal 31
            My Decision Journal for the Facilitator 32
        Decision Continuums 33
            Decision Continuums for the Facilitator 34
        A Time for Everything 35
            A Time for Everything for the Facilitator 36

3. **Types of Consequences and Rewards** 37
    Types of Consequences and Rewards Behavioral Coping Skils 38
        The Consequence of Consequences 39
            The Consequence of Consequences for the Facilitator 40
        Rewards Match Game 41-43
            Rewards Match Game for the Facilitator 44
        I've Got a Secret 45-47
            I've Got a Secret for the Facilitator 48

4. **Dangers** 49
    Dangers Behavioral Coping Skils 50
        Addiction Feud 51
            Addiction Feud for the Facilitator 52
        Recovery Choices 53
            Recovery Choices for the Facilitator 54
        Teenage Undercover Peace Agent 55
            Teenage Undercover Peace Agent for the Facilitator 56
        Food ... Glorious Food – or is it? 57
            Food ... Glorious Food – or is it? for the Facilitator 58

(Continued on the next page)

Introduction

Teens ~ Actions, Consequences, Rewards

TABLE OF CONTENTS *(continued)*

Vehicle Vows - Drive to Dance 59
Vehicle Vows - Passenger Plight..60
Vehicle Vows - Post or Poster?..61
    Vehicle Vows for the Facilitator 62
Sexual Situations – What Could Happen? 63
    Sexual Situations – What Could Happen? for the Facilitator.................64
Self-Harm Help - Emoticon..65
Self-Harm Help - Alternatives..66
Self-Harm Help - Positive Personal Power...67
    Self-Harm for the Facilitator..68
Contemplate My Life 69
    Contemplate My Life for the Facilitator 70
Gang Busters..71
    Gang Busters for the Facilitator..72
Gun Safety Pyramid 73
    Gun Safety Pyramid for the Facilitator...74
Dating Violence Prevention...75
    Dating Violence Prevention for the Facilitator 76
Break the Bullying Cycle - The UN-interrupted Cycle 77
Break the Bullying Cycle - The IN-terrupted Cycle 78
Break the Bullying Cycle - Consequences and Rewards 79
    Break the Bullying Cycle for the Facilitator 80

5. **Attributes**..81
   Attributes Behavioral Coping Skils...82
   Health-A-Gories Part I 83
   Health-A-Gories Part II 84
       Health-A-Gories for the Facilitator 85
   Transparency Game 87
       Transparency Game for the Facilitator...88
   Rebelling? Now, Try Renovating! 89
       Rebelling? Now, Try Renovating! for the Facilitator........................90

6. **Circumstances** 91
   Circumstances Behavioral Coping Skils 92
   FUNction Junction - Rules and Roles Charades..................................93
   FUNction Junction - Self-Affirmations..94
   FUNction Junction - Have FUNction 95
       FUNction Junction for the Facilitator 96
   Everyone is Different from Me, but Can be Similar! 97
       Everyone is Different from Me, but Can be Similar for the Facilitator 98
   Ostrich or Einstein?..99
       Ostrich or Einstein? for the Facilitator 100
   Noble Nobel...101
       Noble Nobel for the Facilitator..102
   Academics - Stress Graph..103
   Academics - Timely Rewards 104

(Continued on the next page)

Teens ~ Actions, Consequences, Rewards
TABLE OF CONTENTS (continued)

    Academics - Techniques 105
        Academics for the Facilitator 106
    You Can Help No Matter What! 107
        You Can Help No Matter What! for the Facilitator 108

7. Rewards 109
  Rewards Behavioral Coping Skills 110
    Hope 111
        Hope for the Facilitator 112
    Mistakes 113
        Mistakes for the Facilitator 114
    Life is 115
        Life is … for the Facilitator 116
    The Glory of Love 117
        The Glory of Love for the Facilitator 118

Recap of Teens ~ Actions, Consequences, Rewards 119
Recap of Teens ~ Actions, Consequences, Rewards Behavioral Coping Skills 120
    Reward Extraordinaire 121-122
    Reward Celebration 123
        Reward Extraordinaire for the Facilitator 124
    Recap – *My Actions Book* 125
    Recap – My Actions Book – Re: *Teens – Actions, Consequences, Rewards* 126
    Recap – My Actions Book – Rewards of a Thing Well Done 127
        Recap – Rewards of a Thing Well Done for the Facilitator 128

Deepest Gratitude to …
the following professionals who make us look good …

Editor and Lifelong Teacher – Eileen Regen, M.Ed., CJE

Reviewers – Annette Damien, MS, PPS
Beth Jennings, CTEC Counselor
Niki Tilicki, MAED

Illustrator – Amy L. Brodsky, LISW-S

Proofreader – Jay Leutenberg, CASA

Art Director – Joy Dey

Assistant Art Director – Mathew Pawlak

Editorial Director – Carlene Sippola

FIRST ACTIVITY

Keep all special thoughts and memories for a lifetime to come. Share these keepsakes with others to inspire hope and build from the past, which can bridge to the future.
~ Mattie Stepanek

FIRST ACTIVITY – MY ACTIONS BOOK .... page 13 ▶
Teens set the stage to save and organize their handouts, art work, journaling and other creations. Teens brainstorm the benefits of journals and scrapbooks to collect memories, insights, actions, consequences and rewards.

First Activity - *My Actions Book* Behavioral Coping Skills

Throughout the First Activity, teens will communicate through oral, written, and artistic expression and give and receive feedback.

Teens: Skills in each activity.
Facilitators: Competencies to evaluate.

First Activity – My Actions Book
- Identify the value of organizing thoughts and work by creating a notebook.
- Demonstrate awareness of upcoming topics by listing them in a Table of Contents.
- Personalize the notebook by adding a sub-title and decorating the cover.
- Demonstrate the importance of *work-in-progress* by adding meaningful items to one's notebook.
- Identify six or more benefits of keeping a journal or scrapbook.

FIRST ACTIVITY - *My Actions Book*

You are about to explore your actions, consequences, and rewards.
You will be creating documents through writing and drawing on handouts, etc.
We suggest that you save them in a three ring or other notebook or scrapbook.
You will add some *fun* sections.

Why organize?

Organizing is what you do before you do something, so that when you do it, it is not all mixed up.

~ A. A. Milne

Let's Get Started

Title your notebook My Actions Book.
   Now or later add your own subtitle.
      Decorate the cover of your book.
         Create a Table of Contents.
            Feel free to add chapters as you discover new topics.
               You may change the order of the chapters, as you wish.

1. Healthy and Unhealthy Risks
2. Decisions
3. Types of Consequences and Rewards
4. Dangers
5. Attributes
6. Circumstances
7. Rewards
8. Recap
9. The Soundtrack of My Life
10. My Future Soundtrack
11. My Favorites
12. My Picture Gallery

- You may wish to label tabs with the topics.
- For each chapter, create a cover page with a quote, written by you or by someone else.
- Safeguard your creations by keeping your book in a secure and private location.
- Your book is a work-in-progress: As you go along, add your journal entries, poems, articles, printouts from websites and whatever relates to your life - actions, consequences and rewards.
- You will look back on them later and recall your experiences during moments in time, and you will be able to notice the changes in yourself and in your life.

TEENS – ACTIONS, CONSEQUENCES, REWARDS

FIRST ACTIVITY - MY ACTIONS BOOK
FOR THE FACILITATOR

I. **Purpose**
   To foster a belief that the upcoming sessions have personal relevance to reflect on.
   To acknowledge that this information is worth preserving.

II. **Skills**
   Identify the value of organizing and recalling thoughts and personal work.
   Demonstrate awareness of upcoming topics by listing them in a Table of Contents.
   Personalize the notebook by adding a subtitle and decorating the cover.
   Demonstrate the importance of work-in-progress by adding meaningful items to the notebook.
   Identify six or more benefits of keeping a journal or scrapbook.

III. **Possible Activities**
   a. The day before the *First Activity* ask teens to bring three ring binders, notebooks or scrapbooks to the session or have these available for teens.
   b. Have color markers available to decorate the book covers.
   c. Distribute the *First Activity – My Actions Book* handout.
   d. A volunteer reads the text at the top and this A. A. Milne quotation aloud: "Organizing is what you do before you do something, so that when you do it, it is not all mixed up."
   e. Direct teens to follow the instructions under *Let's Get Started*.
   f. Allow time for completion.
   g. Encourage teens to share their covers and subtitles and receive peer feedback.

IV. **Enrichment Activities**
   a. Encourage a discussion about teens' experiences with journals and/or scrapbooks.
   b. Prompt teens to brainstorm the value of journals and scrapbooks.
      Possibilities
      - Preserve memories
      - Reflect on what matters most at different moments in time
      - Save original poetry, prose and art
      - Capture moments in time – insights and emotions
      - Re-evaluate own ideas as time passes
      - Provide a bridge between past, present and future self

HEALTHY AND UNHEALTHY RISKS

Accept that all of us can be hurt, that all of us can and surely will at times fail. Other vulnerabilities, like being embarrassed or risking love, can be terrifying, too. I think we should follow a simple rule: if we can take the worst, take the risk.

~ Joyce Brothers

Rate Your Risk Factors .... page 17 ▶
Teens identify personal and environmental factors that lead to unhealthy and healthy risk-taking. Teens describe their future risk-taking intentions.

Risky the Robot .... page 19 ▶
Teens describe reckless responses to daily situations and evaluate the potential consequences. Teens share examples of healthy risks they would like to take and state their reasons.

MY EARLY WARNING SYSTEM .... page 21 ▶
Teens identify their early warning systems and practice these capabilities to resist attractive but harmful risks. Teens develop safe action plans.

Positive Risks .... page 23 ▶
Teens share actions related to positive social, academic, emotional, physical and community risks and state ways to think and act if disappointments occur. Teens compose acrostics with the letters R-I-S-K.

Mind-Set: Sink or Swim .... page 25 ▶
Teens replace thoughts that prevent progress with ideas that promote positive risks. Teens describe personal applications for quotations regarding success, failure and criticism.

REMINDER:
Save completed handouts in "My Actions Book" (see pages 11-14)

Chapter 1 - Healthy and Unhealthy Risks Behavioral Coping Skills

Throughout the chapter, teens will communicate through oral, written and artistic expression and give and receive feedback.

Teens: Skills in each activity.
Facilitators: Competencies to evaluate.

Rate Your Risk Factors
- Check boxes and answer questions to demonstrate emotional identification and environmental awareness.
- Complete self-assessment and decision-making questions.

Risky the Robot
- Depict and describe a robot with the traits of a person who responds impulsively.
- Compare consequences for the robot and the human.

My Early Warning System
- Identify potential dangerous actions and evaluate the probable negative outcomes.
- Describe a safe action plan.

Positive Risks
- Identify positive risks and the related actions.
- State ways to think and act regarding risk-related disappointments.

Mind-Set: Sink or Swim
- Apply the idiom *sink or swim* to one's thoughts.
- State a positive risk to take.
- Match possible discouraging comments with self-motivating rebuttals.

Rate Your Risk-Factors

> **Unhealthy risk** – possible danger that injury, damage or
> loss will occur; potentially life-destroying.

Place a check in the box in front of the statements that apply to you.

Personal
- ☐ I become aggressive when I am angry.
- ☐ I have no academic interests.
- ☐ I lose my inhibitions.
- ☐ I am depressed.
- ☐ I have difficulty getting along with peers.
- ☐ I am easily bored.
- ☐ I am impulsive.
- ☐ I have low self-esteem.
- ☐ I love a thrill.

Environmental
- ☐ I have daredevils as role models.
- ☐ People in my life take dangerous risks.
- ☐ I am frequently exposed to emotionally charged situations.
- ☐ I am frequently exposed to music, games, books, television shows, and movies that glamorize dangerous risk-takers.
- ☐ I have an unstable home – conflict, abuse, etc.

> **Healthy risk** – out of the comfort zone, trying new things,
> not dangerous; potentially life-affirming.

Place a check in the box in front of the statements that apply to you.

Personal
- ☐ I am accountable for my actions and outcomes.
- ☐ I ignore people who say "It can't be done."
- ☐ I ask the opinions of trusted advisors.
- ☐ I analyze pros and cons before deciding.
- ☐ I am eager to face a challenge.
- ☐ I am interested in new ideas.
- ☐ I make informed decisions about possible outcomes.
- ☐ I am motivated more by passion for the activity than by fear of failure.
- ☐ I am willing to try again after disappointments.

Environmental
- ☐ I have people in my life who take positive risks.
- ☐ I have role-models who encourage and/or guide me.
- ☐ I am frequently exposed to music, games, books, television shows, and movies that honor heroes.
- ☐ I admire role models who make the world a better place.
- ☐ I have a stable home atmosphere.

In the past, have you been more likely to take unhealthy or healthy risks? _____

Would you rather take unhealthy or healthy risks in the future? _____

Explain _____

_____

TEENS – ACTIONS, CONSEQUENCES, REWARDS

Rate Your Risk Factors

FOR THE FACILITATOR

I. Purpose
To identify internal and environmental factors that lead to unhealthy and healthy risk-taking. To assess types of risks taken in the past and decide which type is preferred for the future.

II. Skills
Demonstrate skills of emotional identification, environmental awareness, self-assessment and decision-making.

III. Possible Activities
a. Write "Daredevil" on the board and ask teens to brainstorm examples.
   Possibilities
   People who …
   - scale and jump from tall buildings
   - are high-wire performers
   - perform motorcycle jumps and stunts
   - go over Niagara Falls in a barrel or on a tightrope
   - are handcuffed in a box and submerged under water
b. Explain that teens will discover the types of risks they may be likely to take.
c. Distribute the Rate Your *Risk-Factors* handout.
d. A volunteer reads the unhealthy and healthy risk definitions aloud.
e. Explain that this is not a test or a scientific measurement. Tell teens the purpose is to identify personal and environmental factors that may affect risk-taking decisions.
f. Allow time for completion.
g. Ask for a show of hands of teens more likely to take unhealthy risks and those more likely to take healthy risks.
h. Ask each teen to share one statement that was personally applicable.
i. Encourage teens to discuss the type of risks they would rather take in the future and why.
j. Ideally, they will prefer healthy risks but do not argue with those who choose unhealthy risks.
k. Ask "What can unhealthy risk-takers potentially lose?" (life or limb).
l. Ask "What would not meeting a goal mean to a healthy risk-taker?" (The person learned what does, and what does not, work).

IV. Enrichment Activities
a. Encourage discussion and debate regarding:
   Which affects one's type of risk-taking more, personal or environmental factors. Why?
b. Ask teens to research daredevils (sports-people, tightrope walkers, channel swimmers, etc.) Discuss the glamorous side (attention, thrills, etc.) and then the risky side (injuries, months in traction, pain).
c. Continue the session or follow up with the *Risky the Robot* handout, page 19.

Healthy and Unhealthy Risks ▶

Risky the Robot

Risky is a robot that resembles a teen, but Risky was programmed to act on first impulse. Risky responds without thinking, to everything and everyone it meets.

Draw your interpretation of
Risky the Robot

Describe how Risky the Robot would survive in a situation in which a teen might not survive.

_____
_____
_____
_____
_____

What consequences might Risky the Robot face?

_____
_____
_____
_____
_____

What consequences could the teen face?

_____
_____
_____
_____
_____

TEENS – ACTIONS, CONSEQUENCES, REWARDS

Risky the Robot

FOR THE FACILITATOR

I. Purpose
To ascribe to a robot the traits of a person who responds impulsively.
To compare a robot's consequences to human consequences.

II. Skills
Describe reckless responses to daily life situations and evaluate the potential consequences.

III. Possible Activities
a. Before the session, consider providing color paper, scissors and glue. (see "j" below.)
b. Recruit a volunteer to walk into the room acting like a robot (may walk rigidly, speak in a contrived manner, etc.).
c. At the start of the session, the volunteer portrays the robot; teens guess what is being represented.
d. Encourage teens to briefly describe robots they have seen in movies, videos, etc.
e. Ask: "What would a robot encounter in a day in the life of a typical teen?"
f. Encourage teens to brainstorm; a volunteer lists their ideas on the board.
   Possibilities
   - People at home, school, work, in the community
   - School work and homework
   - Technology
   - Alcohol
   - Drugs
   - Cigarettes
   - Relationships
   - Vehicles
g. Ask teens for a few examples of how a robot, who was programmed to act on first impulse, might react to some of the items listed (punch someone it disliked, ignore homework, drink or smoke).
h. Distribute the *Risky the Robot* handout; a volunteer reads the information about Risky aloud.
i. Emphasize that artistic ability and perfect writing skills are not needed for this activity.
j. Prompt teens to use cartoons, caricatures, symbols, collage-type drawings, etc. to express their ideas, or to cut out geometric shapes from the color paper to create their robot.
k. Allow time for completion.
l. Encourage teens to share their drawings and descriptions and receive peer feedback.
   Possibilities
   Robots may
   - Use drugs
   - Sext
   - Drive dangerously

   Responses to the questions at the bottom of the page will be individual.
m. Ask teens to share ways their robots resemble people they know and themselves.
n. Pose the question "How do the robot's consequences compare to human consequences?" Elicit that the robot is a piece of machinery that can be replaced; people cannot be replaced.

IV. Enrichment Activities
a. Ask teens for examples of healthy risks (try out for a team; learn a new skill; ask someone to go on a date).
b. Distribute poster or plain paper and color markers.
c. Ask teens to depict and describe a robot that takes healthy risks.
d. Encourage teens to share their drawings and receive peer feedback.
e. Ask teens which of their robot's risks they would they like to take and why.

Healthy and Unhealthy Risks

MY EARLY WARNING SYSTEM

A region in your brain can warn you in advance when a behavior might lead to negative outcomes.
Yes, it alerts you to oncoming traffic, but …
Tune into a more subtle risk.

My Early Warning System monitors my environmental cues.

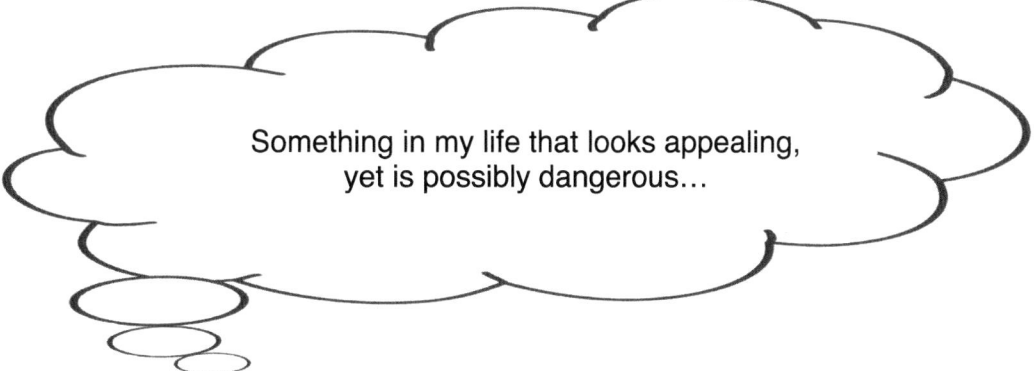

Something in my life that looks appealing, yet is possibly dangerous…

My Early Warning System weighs my possible negative outcomes.

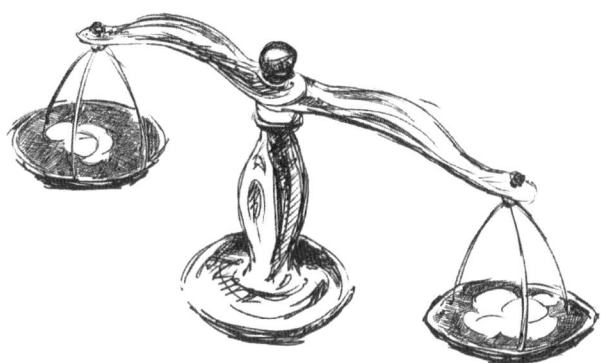

My possible negative outcomes …

My Early Warning System helps me adjust my behavior to avoid danger.

My actions will be…

_____

_____

_____

MY EARLY WARNING SYSTEM

FOR THE FACILITATOR

I. Purpose
To identify the functions of the brain's early warning system.
To practice these capabilities concerning a current attractive but harmful risk.

II. Skills
State potential dangers, evaluate probable negative outcomes and plan safe actions.

III. Possible Activities
   a. Recruit a volunteer to draw on the board; whisper a request to draw a traffic light.
   b. Ask teens the purpose of red, yellow and green lights. (Stop, caution or slowdown, go).
   c. Explain that brains have similar safety systems.
   d. Distribute the *My Early Warning System* handout; a volunteer reads the top four lines aloud.
   e. Emphasize that teens are to write about something dangerous they could be tempted to do.
   f. Allow time for completion.
   g. Encourage teens to share their responses and receive peer feedback.
   Possibilities
   Something in my life that looks appealing, yet is possibly dangerous ...
   - Alcohol, drugs, cigarettes
   - Face-to-face or online bullying, gossiping, discrimination, judgmental remarks
   - Gambling, stealing
   - Lying, manipulating, cheating
   - Unsafe sex, pressuring someone to have sex, sexting
   - Posting or sending photos

   My possible negative outcomes ...
   - Damage to physical and emotional health; one's own or another's death
   - Guilt from inflicting invisible wounds on others through bullying, etc.
   - Juvenile justice system
   - Reputation as untrustworthy, cruel, bigoted
   - Unwanted pregnancy, legal charges, physical and emotional harm to oneself and others

   My actions will be ...
   - Avoid unhealthy substances
   - Treat others as I want to be treated
   - Earn money in honest ways
   - Tell the truth, ask for what I want, never cheat people out of money, never cheat on tests
   - Make sexual decisions based on both partners' values, safety, and health considerations

IV. Enrichment Activities
   a. Ask teens why an emergency vehicle cannot be missed. (Flashing lights, bells and whistles).
   b. Pose the question "Why do we sometimes miss messages from an internal warning system?"
   Possibilities
   - They're not always as loud and clear as a siren
   - They may be heard as a still, small voice
   - We may wish to ignore them due to the deceptive appeal of the danger
   c. Ask teens what traffic rules apply to their Early Warning System. (Stop, look and listen; wait for the green light; ignore distractions; pay attention to warning signs, etc.).
   d. Present the possibilities ("g" above) that were not addressed to the group. Discuss what the "early warnings" look like for each situation.

Healthy and Unhealthy Risks ▶

Positive Risks

Social	**Social**	**Social**	**School**	**School**
Reach out to a new friend.	Try to clear up a misunderstanding.	Approach someone about going out.	Accept an academic challenge.	Take on an athletic challenge.
How?	How?	How?	How?	How?
If I am rejected?	If it doesn't work?	If I am told "no"?	If the goal is not met?	If I'm not successful?

School	**Emotional**	**Emotional**	**Emotional**	**Physical**
Run for an office.	Share feelings.	Ask for help.	Begin to recover.	Celebrate a trait.
How?	How?	How?	How?	How?
If I lose?	If my feelings are not understood?	If it is not helpful?	If it's painful?	If I am criticized?

Physical	**Physical**	**Community**	**Community**	**Community**
Try a new style	Join an exercise class.	Volunteer to help others.	Mentor young children.	Start a business or charity.
How?	How?	How?	How?	How?
If it is not comfortable?	If it is not gratifying?	If it is not the right fit?	If it's not enjoyable?	If it doesn't work out?

Positive Risks

FOR THE FACILITATOR

I. **Purpose**
To identify positive risks that will benefit teens.
To describe the actions involved in taking the risks.
To describe ways to think and act regarding risk-related disappointments.

II. **Skills**
Answer game questions that promote growth regarding social, school-related, physical, and community risks.
Compose positive risk situations.
Describe ways to handle unfavorable outcomes.

III. **Possible Activities**
  a. Before the session, photocopy and cut the *Positive Risk* handout on the broken lines.
  b. Place the cutouts face down on a table at the front of the room.
  c. Cut blank strips of paper, (adequate size for a sentence), one per participant; set aside.
  d. At the start of the session, ask teens for examples of risky sports (hang gliding, rock climbing).
  e. Ask for examples of high risk occupations (astronaut, deep sea explorer).
  f. Explain that teens will play a game about positive risks that are not dangerous that teens can take daily.
  g. Describe the game play: "When it's your turn, go to the front of the room, pick up a cutout and read the risk aloud."
     - Call on volunteers to respond to the "How" question and the "If …" question.
     - "How" relates to actions that carry out the risk.
     - "If …" relates to positive ways to think and act if the outcome is disappointing."
  h. Put an example on the board: "Risk – Initiate a new sport at school." (*Elicit: pole-vaulting, ice-skating, etc.*).
     - "How?" (*Elicit: start with a petition, talk with the physical education teacher, research costs, etc.*).
     - "What if you are turned down?" (*Elicit: be glad you tried, approach other resources e.g. the Department of Parks and Recreation, etc.*).
  i. Teens play the game until all cutouts are used.
  j. Distribute blank strips of paper.
  k. Encourage each teen to write any positive risk on the strip of paper.
  l. Collect the strips of paper and place face down at the front of the room.
  m. Teens take turns reading risks aloud, calling on volunteers to share actions they would take and the positive thoughts and reactions they would use to handle unwanted outcomes.

IV. **Enrichment Activities**
Write the word *RISK* vertically on the board and prompt teens to form an acrostic.
  Possibilities
    R – Right timing
    I – Intelligent risk
    S – See the possibilities
    K – Know what could be lost and gained

Healthy and Unhealthy Risks ▶

Mind-Set: Sink or Swim

Your mind-set is your outlook on the world and your *in-look* at yourself.
Regarding risks, your mind-set can influence whether you sink or swim.

Place the letter of the corresponding swim thought in front of each *sink* thought.	
Sink *(failure)* **Thoughts**	**Swim** *(success)* **Thoughts**
_____ 1. I'll look foolish if I try and fail.	A. Not being successful is not trying.
_____ 2. People will laugh at me.	B. I can learn from successful people.
_____ 3. I'll be disappointed if it doesn't work out.	C. I benefit from useful criticism.
	D. I can jump in with both feet.
_____ 4. If I fail I'm a failure.	E. I'd be foolish if I didn't try.
_____ 5. I have no talent.	F. I'll take smart risks.
_____ 6. They say I'm not realistic.	G. I can survive disappointments.
_____ 7. I can back out.	H. I'll be smiling at my bravery
_____ 8. I can't take criticism.	I. I say I'm optimistic.
_____ 9. I'll play it safe to look smart.	J. I have talent in my passion and work ethics.
_____ 10. I'm threatened by others' successes.	
_____ 11. People will never forget what I did.	K. I will move forward.

Replace thoughts that prevent progress with thoughts that promote positive risks.

A positive risk I'd like to take is …

People could try to discourage me by saying …

My own sinking (unsuccessful) thoughts could tell me …

To swim (succeed) I'll tell myself …

Mind-Set: Sink or Swim

FOR THE FACILITATOR

I. Purpose
To replace thoughts that prevent progress with thoughts that promote positive risks.

II. Skills
Apply the idiom *sink or swim* to thoughts.
State a positive risk to take.
Quote possible discouraging comments and formulate self-motivating statements.
Demonstrate mind-set insights by responding to quotations and questions.

III. Possible Activities
   a. Write "Sink or swim" on the board and elicit its meaning. (Fail or succeed).
   b. Ask teens the meaning of healthy or positive risks. (Opportunities for progress, challenges).
   c. Explain that teens will replace *sink* thoughts with *swim* thoughts regarding healthy risks.
   d. Distribute the *Mind-Set: Sink or Swim* handout; a volunteer reads the explanation at the top of the page.
   e. Allow time for completion.
   f. Encourage teens to share responses and receive peer feedback.
   Possibilities
   Suggested answer key

| E – 1 | H – 2 | G – 3 | A – 4 | J – 5 | I – 6 | D – 7 | C – 8 | F – 9 | B – 10 | K – 11 |

   Sentence starter responses will be individual.

IV. Enrichment Activities
   a. Write the following quote on the board:
   "When you take risks you learn that there will be times when you succeed and there will be times when you fail, and both are equally important." ~ *Ellen DeGeneres*
   b. Encourage teens to respond to these prompts:
      - Share times when you took a risk and succeeded.
      - Share times when you took a risk and did not succeed.
      - Why are both equally important? (Learn what does and does not work, etc.).
   c. Write the following quote on the board:
   "There is only one way to avoid criticism: do nothing, say nothing, and be nothing." ~ *Aristotle*
   d. Encourage teens to answer the related questions aloud.
      - Tell about a time you wanted to do something but didn't do it to avoid criticism.
      - Share an opinion you wanted to express (no put-downs) but didn't do it to avoid criticism.
      - If you knew you would not be criticized, what productive action would you take?
      - Give an opinion about a controversial issue (no put-downs); peers are not allowed to criticize.
      - Describe something or someone you will be if you stop fearing criticism.
      - Which is worse – criticism from others or from yourself? Why?
   e. Encourage teens to individually or in teams compose their own healthy risk-related mind-set quotes.
   f. Write "Replace thoughts that prevent progress with thoughts that promote positive risks" on the board.
   g. Ask a volunteer to draw a target below the sentence with large arrows pointing to the target.
   h. Teens take turns stating a negative thought aloud.
   i. For each negative thought, a teen writes a positive replacement on one of the arrows that point to the target.

DECISIONS 2

It's not hard to decide what you want your life to be about. What's hard... is figuring out what you're willing to give up in order to do the things you really care about.
~ Shauna Niequist

Stop and Think .... page **29** ▶
Teens create scenarios in which impulsivity causes negative outcomes. Teens practice five decision-making steps and describe the potential positive outcomes.

My Decision-Making Journal .... page **31** ▶
Teens apply concepts related to the words decision, detour, deception, denial, dilemma, dream and delay to a fictional person's journal. Teens personalize these concepts and answer related questions.

Decision Continuums .... page **33** ▶
Teens rate what influenced a recent decision on eight scales and describe its outcomes. Teens describe what they do and do not want and the corresponding decisions.

A Time for Everything .... page **35** ▶
Teens identify times to respect impulses and times for more thoughtful choices. Teens share examples of their impulsive, and more thoughtful, decisions and their outcomes.

REMINDER:
Save completed handouts in "My Actions Book" (see pages 11-14)

Chapter 2 - Decisions Behavioral Coping Skills

Throughout the chapter, teens will communicate through oral, written and creative expression and give and receive feedback.

Teens: Skills in each activity.
Facilitators: Competencies to evaluate.

Stop and Think
- Imagine and describe a main character who acts impulsively and experiences negative outcomes.
- Rewrite the scene to show the character using five decision-making steps.
- Identify the person's options and rate each as likely to produce positive or negative outcomes.

My Decision-Making Journal
- Fill in the blanks of a fictitious person's journal using "D" words related to decisions.
- Create a personal journal entry using the seven "D" words related to an upcoming decision.

Decision Continuums
- Describe a major decision recently made.
- Rate what influenced the decision on eight scales.
- Describe positive outcomes wanted and the decisions that help promote the rewards.
- Describe negative outcomes to be avoided and the decisions that help prevent the consequences.

A Time for Everything
- Read ten situations, each with two possible decisions.
- Select ten decisions believed to be the best.
- Identify which of the best decisions are based on impulse and which are based on thought.
- Give examples of decisions and identify types and outcomes.

Decisions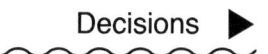

Stop and Think

**Create a fictional scenario in which a teen experiences a negative outcome caused by impulsive actions and lack of forethought.
Your main character can be a perpetrator or a potential victim.**

Dream up your own topic or choose from this list below:

Alcohol and/or Drugs	Bullying	Cheating
Emotional, Physical, Sexual and/or Verbal Abuse	Gossiping	Harm to self
Harm to others	Lying	Stealing

My Fictional Scenario

Now, rewrite a plan for your fictional scenario, using these decision-making steps below.

STOP: When was the ideal time to stop and apply *mental brakes*?

_____

THINK OF OPTIONS: What could the person have thought about to prevent a negative outcome?

_____

IDENTIFY OPTIONS and their most likely negative and/or positive outcomes:

1. _____
2. _____
3. _____
4. _____

GUESSTIMATE OUTCOMES
Place an "N" in front of options with probable **negative** outcomes.
Place a "P" in front of options with probable **positive** outcomes.

PLAN – What would be the best plan to achieve a positive outcome?

_____

TEENS – ACTIONS, CONSEQUENCES, REWARDS

Stop and Think

FOR THE FACILITATOR

I. Purpose
To practice steps in decision-making by examining forethought versus impulsivity.

II. Skills
Create a scenario in which a teen experiences negative outcomes due to acting without thinking. Practice five steps the main character could have taken to achieve positive outcomes.

III. Possible Activities
a. Ask teens to describe movies, books or news events in which young people have been hurt physically or emotionally.
b. Pose the question "What can happen when people speak or act without thinking?" (Possible physical or emotional harm).
c. Distribute the *Stop and Think* handout; a volunteer reads the directions and the list aloud.
d. Encourage teens to brainstorm other topics as the facilitator lists them on the board.
e. Ask teens to write a fictional scenario in the box and continue with the decision-making process at the bottom of the page.
f. Allow time for completion.
g. Encourage teens to share their scenarios and responses to the decision-making process, and receive peer feedback.
h. Ask teens to identify the step they think is most important and explain why. (Individualized responses).

IV. Enrichment Activities
a. Separate teens into small improvisational theater casts.
b. The actors meet in clusters to create their scenarios in which teens need to stop and think and briefly practice their parts.
c. The group re-convenes and actors begin to portray their scenarios.
d. The scenes will not conclude with negative outcomes because the audience will intervene.
e. The audience members become the coaches, and use the decision-making steps listed on their handouts.
f. Audience coaches take turns at appropriate times and shout out:
   - Stop
   - Think
   - Identify options
   - Guesstimate outcomes
   - Plan
g. The actors respond to the coaches' prompts verbally.
h. After all scenarios are performed and coached, debrief with these questions:
   - "How did it feel to be helped through the decision-making process?"
   - "How will coaching others help you coach yourself?"

Decisions

My Decision-Making Journal

Use the word bank to complete the entry.

| decision   detour   deceiving   denial   dilemma   dream   delay |

Dear Journal,

I am dating a really cool person who is good-looking and popular.
My friends say I am in _____ about the truth.
My partner flirts a lot but it doesn't mean anything.
My partner just has an outgoing personality.
Am I _____ myself?
When we argue, my partner sometimes pushes me around.
My friends say to break up.
I guess I'm in a _____.
I don't want to make a _____.
I just can't give up the love of my life.
If I _____ long enough my partner will change.
I'll take a _____ in my mind.
I'll _____ about the good times.

Use the same "D" words to describe a decision you need to make.

Dear Journal,

My Decision-Making Journal

FOR THE FACILITATOR

I. Purpose
To encourage journaling while applying concepts that begin with "D" to decisions.

II. Skills
Apply seven concepts related to decisions by filling in the blanks of a fictitious person's journal.
Personalize the ideas by writing a journal entry.
Demonstrate understanding by answering nine questions in writing or aloud.

III. Possible Activities
a. Ask for a show of hands among teens who have written in journals.
b. Encourage teens to discuss the benefits of journaling (Express thoughts and feelings, gain insight).
c. Distribute the *My Decision-Making* handout; a volunteer reads the directions and the "D" words aloud.
d. Allow time for completion.
e. Review the responses. (Suggested order – denial, deceiving, dilemma, decision, delay, detour, dream).
f. Ask for volunteers to read their own journal entries aloud and receive peer feedback.
g. Assess comprehension by asking the questions below.
Teens may write responses on the back of the handout or answer aloud.
Possible responses are italicized.
- Why would people be in denial?
  They don't want to face the truth.
- How do people deceive themselves?
  They make excuses for others, themselves or situations.
- What is a dilemma?
  A situation necessitating a choice between two possibly undesirable alternatives.
- Why would people NOT want to make a decision?
  Unsure of what to do; afraid to make the wrong decision; know what to do but don't want to do it.
- When is it advisable to delay making a decision?
  In the heat of anger; when one needs more information; when asking trusted people makes sense.
- When is it not advisable to delay making a decision?
  When a situation will worsen or is dangerous; when instincts or trusted advisors say "NOW."
- Why would people take a "mind-detour"?
  To avoid making a decision they don't want to make.
- How could daydreaming help?
  Explore options and outcomes in one's mind.
- How could daydreaming negatively impact the decision-making process?
  Focus on wishes or fantasy rather than the facts.

IV. Enrichment Activities
a. Encourage teens individually or in teams to brainstorm positive decision-related words and phrases that start with A, B and C. They will then have the A, B, C, D's of decision-making!
   Examples
   A words – (examples: admit, awareness, ask advisors, analyze, acceptance, action)
   B words – (examples: beware, brainstorm, be mindful, best option, be open-minded)
   C words – (examples: choices, challenges, consider consequences, confer, counselor, change, chance)
b. Encourage teens to write their own positive decision-making journal entries.

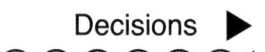

Decision Continuums

Describe a major decision you made recently _____
_____
_____

Place an "X" on each continuum to show what affected this particular decision.

Impulsivity   **Caution**
0---5--10

Feelings   **Rational thoughts**
0---5--10

My wants   **Others' wants**
0---5--10

Independence   **Dependence**
0---5--10

Self-approval   **Others' approval**
0---5--10

Accepted   **Excluded**
0---5--10

Power   **Powerlessness**
0---5--10

Freedom   **Restriction**
0---5--10

What was the major factor that influenced your decision? _____
_____
_____

What were the negative outcomes (if any)? _____
_____

What were the positive outcomes (if any)? _____
_____

Would you make the same decision again? _____ Explain _____
_____

TEENS – ACTIONS, CONSEQUENCES, REWARDS

Decision Continuums

FOR THE FACILITATOR

I. **Purpose**
   To identify motivations and outcomes. To demonstrate goal-oriented decision-making skills.

II. **Skills**
   State a major personal decision.
   Rate the factors that influenced the decision on eight continuums.
   Describe the decision's positive and negative outcomes.
   Decide whether it's advisable to make the decision again and explain why.
   List personal wants and the related decisions.
   List what to avoid and the related decisions.
   Compose short stories about teens in decision-making situations.
   Show on a continuum how the main character in peers' stories was influenced by each factor.

III. **Possible Activities**
   a. Copy this continuum onto the board:
      "Love sports _____Don't care about sports"
   b. Ask a few volunteers to place their initials on the continuum to show their feelings toward sports.
   c. Copy this continuum onto the board:
      "The present moment _____The future"
   d. Ask a few volunteers to place their initials on the continuum to show what drives their decisions.
   e. Distribute the *Decision Continuums* handout; a volunteer reads the directions aloud.
   f. Allow time for completion.
   g. Encourage teens to share their responses and receive peer feedback.
   h. Prompt teens to discuss other factors that influence their decisions. (Peer or parental pressure, etc.).

IV. **Enrichment Activity**
   a. Copy this table onto the board.
   b. Encourage teens to brainstorm responses. A peer lists their ideas on the board.
      A few possibilities are listed.

What I WANT	Decisions to OBTAIN What I WANT
Fun	Find legal and safe enjoyment.
Independence	Work part-time.
More time with friends.	Do homework first.
More control over my life.	Choose my career based on my passion.

   c. Copy this table onto the board.
   d. Encourage teens to brainstorm responses. A peer lists their ideas on the board.
      A few possibilities are listed.

What I DON'T Want	Decisions to AVOID What I DON'T Want
Arguments with parents/caregivers	Use conflict resolution skills.
Social drama	Change the subject when someone gossips.
Loss of privileges	Obey the rules.
Adults telling me what to do	Complete chores before being hounded.

   e. List words on the left side of the handout on the left side of the board the others on the right.
   f. Ask individuals or teams to compose short stories about teens in decision-making situations.
   g. Teens read their stories aloud. Peers move to stand on the left or right side of the room or any point in between to show how the main character was influenced by each factor.
   h. Continue the session or follow with *A Time for Everything?* handout, page 35.

Decisions

A Time for Everything

There are times to follow your first impulse, and times to first think rationally before you act.

For each situation place a check in front of the statement you think is best.

You are in extreme danger and your *fight or flight* response has kicked in.

_____1. Go with your impulse and run!

_____2. Contemplate carefully for ten minutes.

Your feelings say "I'm in love"; your thoughts say "It's infatuation."

_____3. Feelings rule. Commit to an exclusive relationship NOW!

_____4. Honor your thoughts and feelings. Get to know the person better.

You value your independence but are in a crisis and need help.

_____ 5. Prove you can handle it alone.

_____ 6. Recognize that it's a sign of strength to ask for help.

You sit near a person you really like who wants to cheat during a test.

_____ 7. Stick to your beliefs and say "No."

_____ 8. Say "Yes" and hope it will lead to a relationship.

You want to go out with friends; your ill grandfather wants you to visit.

_____ 9. Your wants matter most. Go with your friends.

_____ 10. Your grandfather needs you. Your friends can wait.

You want to do one thing and your friend wants to do something else.

_____ 11. Be a good friend. Give in.

_____ 12. Try for a win-win compromise.

You value your freedom; trusted people suggest a rehabilitation program with lots of restrictions.

_____ 13. Accept temporary restriction for anticipated freedom from your addiction.

_____ 14. No one can tell you what to do. Forget the program.

Dancing is your passion and you have been accepted into a post-high school performing arts program.

_____ 15. Listen to everyone's advice to "Think of the future; choose a more realistic career."

_____ 16. Seize the moment! Jump into the program with both feet and your whole heart.

You are in a power struggle about something that doesn't matter that much to you.

_____ 17. Don't give up your power. Insist on your way.

_____ 18. Give in because the issue matters more to the other person.

People you want as friends ask you to divert a cashier's attention while they shoplift.

_____ 19. You already have an adrenaline rush. You want their acceptance. Do it!

_____ 20. Use your brain. You could get in big trouble. Do you want really want these people as *friends*?

TEENS – ACTIONS, CONSEQUENCES, REWARDS

A Time for Everything

FOR THE FACILITATOR

I. Purpose
To identify times when impulses are to be respected and times for more thoughtful choices.

II. Skills
Read ten situations, each with two possible decisions.
Select a decision believed to be the best for each of ten situations.
Identify which of the best decisions are based on impulse and which are based on thought.
Describe different situations in which teens could choose to follow first impulses or think rationally.
Share personal choices in response to peers' situations.
Show whether each response is based on thoughts or impulses by standing in front of an applicable symbol.

III. Possible Activities
a. Ask teens what they would do if the building were on fire. (Run out!)
b. Ask teens what they would do if a casual acquaintance proposed marriage. (Get to know the person better). Elicit that there are times to follow first impulses and times to first think carefully.
c. Distribute the *A Time for Everything* handout; a volunteer reads the information and directions aloud.
d. Allow time for completion.
e. Encourage teens to share their responses and receive peer feedback.
   Possibilities
   The preferred statements are: 1, 4, 6, 7, 10, 12, 13, 16, 18, 20.
f. Ask teens to identify which of the preferred responses are based on impulse and which are based on thought, and why.
   Possibilities
   1. Impulse – impulsivity means survival in a *fight or flight* moment.
   4. Thought – both thoughts and feelings are respected.
   6. Thought – dependence on a trusted adult in a crisis may make the difference of life or death.
   7. Thought – self-approval is more important than a potential relationship with a cheater.
   10. Thought – this is a time to think about your grandfather's needs.
   12. Thought – compromise balances of both people's wishes.
   13. Thought – external restriction is necessary until one gains internal control and coping skills.
   16. Impulse – the present matters most when one's passion, talent and opportunity coincide.
   18. Thought – to give up power on unimportant issues means to pick one's battles.
   20. Thought – thoughts trump feelings; to be excluded by these so-called friends beats their acceptance.

IV. Enrichment Activities
a. Ask teens to give examples of their own impulsive decisions and the outcomes.
b. Ask teens to give examples of their own thoughtful decisions and the outcomes.
c. Ask volunteers to draw a symbol for *Thought* on one side of the board (brain, lightbulb, etc.) and a symbol for *Impulse* on the other side of the board (wrecking ball, explosion, etc.).
d. Direct individuals or teams to write brief descriptions of situations in which a teen could choose to follow a first impulse or to think rationally first.
e. Teens write only the situations, not the choices.
f. Teens read their situations aloud.
g. For each situation, a few peers describe what they would do, and show whether the choice is based on thought or impulse by standing in front of the applicable symbol.

TYPES OF CONSEQUENCES AND REWARDS

*While we are free to choose our actions,
we are not free to choose the consequences of our actions.*
~ Stephen Covey

The Consequence of Consequences .... page **39** ▶
Teens define external, internal and natural consequences and identify which are illustrated in twenty situations. Teens share personal or fictitious situations and state the types of consequences.

REWARDS MATCH GAME .... page **41-43** ▶
Teens link positive actions with their corresponding rewards and identify rewards as external, internal or natural. Teens state rewards they imagine or have experienced and identify their types.

I've Got a Secret .... page **45-47** ▶
Teens differentiate between apparent and actual rewards and consequences. Teens compose scenarios, state what they would do in the situations, and describe overt and covert consequences and rewards.

REMINDER:
Save completed handouts in "My Actions Book" (see pages 11-14)

Chapter 3 - Types of Consequences and Rewards Behavioral Coping Skills

Throughout the chapter, teens will communicate through oral, written and creative expression and give and receive feedback.

Teens: Skills in each activity.
Facilitators: Competencies to evaluate.

The Consequence of Consequences
- Share a personal consequence and/or listen to peers share their situations.
- State a consequence for each of twenty situations in which teens might experience a negative outcome.
- Label twenty consequences as external, internal or natural after reviewing the definitions.
- Identify five or more types of events not under teens' control that result in consequences.
- Discuss seven or more ways to handle consequences resulting from causes not under personal control.

Rewards Match Game
- Match twenty actions with related rewards.
- State rewards and identify the types of rewards that peers describe during a Reward Go Round.

I've Got a Secret
- Identify fifteen genuine consequences from actions that gain superficial rewards.
- Identify thirteen genuine rewards from actions that appear to result in negative outcomes.
- State what to do in peer-created scenarios.
- Differentiate between the superficial and deeper consequences and rewards of actions.

Types of Consequences and Rewards ▶

The Consequence of Consequences

Add a potential consequence for each statement below:

1. You break curfew. _____
2. You get caught cheating. _____
3. You flirt with your best friend's partner. _____
4. You text while driving. _____
5. You drink. _____
6. You lie to your parents/caregivers. _____
7. You shout obscenities on the playing field. _____
8. You miss work. _____
9. You steal. _____
10. You exaggerate an accomplishment. _____
11. You do something dangerous. _____
12. You sext. _____
13. You spread gossip. _____
14. You buy things you cannot afford. _____
15. You text till late in the night. _____
16. You go on a starvation diet. _____
17. You witness bullying and are silent. _____
18. You drive too fast. _____
19. You betray a friend's confidentiality. _____
20. You don't study for a test. _____

Consequence = a negative outcome

E = External Consequence = enforced from the outside: (break laws – go to jail)

I = Internal Consequence = felt from the inside: (cheat – feel guilty)

N = Natural Consequence = resultant from the action: (touch fire – get burned)

In front of each number above write an E, I and/or N to identify the type of consequence.

TEENS – ACTIONS, CONSEQUENCES, REWARDS

The Consequence of Consequences

FOR THE FACILITATOR

I. Purpose
To identify potential consequences and their types.

II. Skills
Share a personal consequence and/or listen to peers share their situations.
State a consequence for each of twenty situations in which teens might experience a negative outcome.
Label twenty consequences as external, internal or natural after reviewing the definitions.
Identify five or more types of events not under teens' control that result in consequences.
Discuss seven or more ways to handle consequences resulting from causes not under personal control.

III. Possible Activities
a. Encourage a brief discussion of situations in which teens have experienced consequences.
b. Explain that teens will consider three different types of consequences.
c. Distribute the *The Consequence of Consequences* handout.
d. Review the directions and definitions with the group.
e. Allow time for completion.
f. Encourage teens to share their responses and receive peer feedback.
Possibilities
- Expect a variety of individual responses for the consequences and their types.
- Encourage teens to discuss and debate the types of consequences based on the definitions.

IV. Enrichment Activities
a. Ask "Which of the twenty consequences on the handout were preventable?" (All).
b. Prompt teens to brainstorm events that cause consequences that are not under teens' control.
Possibilities
- A tsunami or other acts of nature.
- A plane crash or accident that is not a teen's fault.
- The illness of family and friends.
- The death of a loved one.
- The unwanted break up of a friendship or romance.
- A family financial loss, separation or divorce, addiction, domestic violence or abuse.

c. Encourage a discussion about ways to handle family crises and other tragedies.
Possibilities
- Express feelings – cry, talk, write, draw, etc.
- Engage in diversions – movies, books, sports, etc.
- Seek support – friends, family, medical or mental health professionals, spiritual advisors, etc.
- Help with relief efforts in disasters – distribute food and supplies, volunteer at a shelter, etc.
- Do not blame self – the situation was not under personal control.
- Work on forgiveness – if someone else was responsible.
- Avoid survivor guilt – for living through a catastrophe in which others died or suffered.

Rewards Match Game

Cut out the boxes.
Scramble the cutouts.
For the Match Game, distribute the cutouts; people with **A** and **R** cutouts find their matches.
For the Individual Puzzle, individuals match the each (A) Action with its (R) Reward cutout.

A I work hard in school and pass all my courses.	**R** I graduate.	**A** I drive safely.	**R** I am trusted to drive.
A I eat healthy food.	**R** My food-plan works.	**A** I exercise daily.	**R** I have a strong body.
A I say "No" to my friend's partner.	**R** I consider myself to be loyal.	**A** I do my job well.	**R** I get a raise.

(Continued on the next page)

TEENS – ACTIONS, CONSEQUENCES, REWARDS

REWARDS MATCH GAME (Continued)

A	R	A	R
I obey laws.	I do not worry when I see the police.	I speak out against bigotry.	I'm glad I fight discrimination.
A I make an appropriate but funny video.	**R** People laugh.	**A** I change the subject when people gossip.	**R** I'm proud to do my part to stop slander.
A I control my spending.	**R** I am not in debt.	**A** I avoid alcohol and drugs.	**R** I am in control of my thoughts and actions.
A I am an advocate for someone who is bullied.	**R** I am a caring person.	**A** I ask for help with a problem.	**R** I am able to acknowledge my needs.

(Continued on the next page)

Rewards Match Game *(Continued)*

A	R	A	R
I tell the truth when I'd rather lie.	I value my honesty.	I say "No" when I'd rather say "Yes."	I know when refusal is right for me.
I wipe up a slippery floor.	I feel good about preventing a fall.	I play by the team's rules.	I get to stay in the game.
I write a controversial essay.	I feel good getting my point across to others.	I am a volunteer.	I feel great by giving back.

TEENS – ACTIONS, CONSEQUENCES, REWARDS

REWARDS MATCH GAME

FOR THE FACILITATOR

I. Purpose
To match positive actions with probable rewards.
To identify the types of rewards.

II. Skills
Match twenty positive actions to their corresponding rewards.
Identify each reward as one or more of the following: external, internal or natural.

III. Possible Activities
a. Before the session:
- Decide which format below to use and make the appropriate number of photocopies.
- Obtain enough scissors for teens to share if the Individual Puzzle Format is used.
- Print a picture of a medal or trophy or recruit an artistic teen to draw one.

b. At the start of the session, show the picture and ask teens what it represents. (A win or an honor).

c. Tell teens they will play a game about rewards.

d. For any format, encourage teens to compose two actions and two corresponding consequences in the blank boxes of page 43.

Match Game Format
- Make one set of cutouts.
- Distribute "A" Action cards to half of the teens and "R" Reward cards to the other half.
- Teens with Action cutouts take turns at the front of the room and read aloud one action per turn.
- For each action, the teen with the corresponding Reward cutout reads it aloud.
- If more than one teen say they hold the matching reward, consider substantiated responses correct.

Individual Puzzle Format
- Distribute the *Rewards Match Game* handouts and scissors.
- Tell teens to:
  Cut out the boxes and scramble the cutouts.
  Match each (A) Action cutout with its corresponding (R) Reward cutout.
- Encourage teens to share their responses.

Answer Key for either format
The uncut handout is the answer key – the matching actions and rewards are next to each other.

IV. Enrichment Activities
a. Write the types of rewards on the board:
"External – received from the outside; Internal – felt from the inside; Natural – results from the action."

b. Teens take turns reading Rewards cutouts aloud as volunteers identify its type.
- The possible types of rewards are shown below; consider any substantiated responses correct.
- Reward types are shown in the order of the handouts – left to right, top to bottom; key words for each reward box are noted for ease. Some rewards have more than one type of reward.

Graduate – E, N	Raise – E	Debt – E, N	Refusal – I
Drive – E	Obey – I	Thoughts – N	Preventing – I
Eat – N	Discrimination – I	Caring – I	Game – E, N
Exercise – N	Laugh – E	Acknowledge – I	Writing – I
Loyal – I	Slander – I	Honesty – I	Volunteer – I

c. Initiate a Reward-Go-Round
- Teens stand or sit in a circle.
- Teens take turns stating rewards (ones they have experienced or can imagine).
- Peers identify each reward as External, Internal or Natural.

I've Got a Secret

Game Show Host Instructions
Call on one contestant per question.
Read the first three lines. Allow time to respond.
Accept any reasonable response.
After each contestant's turn, you may read the italicized text aloud
if it's different from the response.

1. I ace the test because I cheat.
   My teacher compliments me and my parents are thrilled.
   What's my secret consequence?
   I feel guilty.

2. I get a "C" in the course because I didn't cheat.
   It will drop my GPA (Grade Point Average).
   What's my secret reward?
   I am honest.

3. My dating partner adores me because I go along with everything.
   We never argue.
   What's my secret consequence?
   I am not true to myself.

4. My dating partner breaks up with me because I don't go along with everything.
   I listen open-mindedly but then share my views.
   What's my secret reward?
   I honor my beliefs.

5. My friends laugh at my joke about someone.
   I feel like now I really belong to this group.
   What's my secret consequence?
   My acceptance to the group is at someone else's expense.

6. My friends act cold toward me when I stick up for someone who is different.
   They may not want to be my friends.
   What's my secret reward?
   I advocate for people's rights.

7. My co-worker skips work to go to a big game.
   I work and miss the big game.
   What's my secret reward?
   I take pride in being responsible.

8. I tell my boss I am sick so I can go to a party.
   My boss shows real concern about me.
   What's my secret consequence?
   I know I have lied.

9. I take performance enhancing drugs.
   I make the team.
   What's my secret consequence?
   My real abilities didn't get me here.

(Continued on the next page)

TEENS – ACTIONS, CONSEQUENCES, REWARDS

I've Got a Secret *(Continued)*

10. I practice hard every day.
    I don't make the team.
    What's my secret reward?

    I know I did my best.

11. I look great at the beach.
    I go to extremes to be very thin.
    What's my secret consequence?

    I am tortured by an eating disorder.

12. A lot of people have bodies like jocks or movie stars.
    I eat healthy foods and exercise but know I won't look the same.
    What's my secret reward?

    I accept my body build.

13. I work a lot of extra hours to afford the best.
    I am accepted by people with money.
    What's my secret consequence?

    I am accepted for what I have, not who I am.

14. I have a few loyal friends.
    We are not in a clique that excludes others.
    What's my secret reward?

    I have true friends who are honorable.

15. People I want as friends love violent lyrics.
    I pretend to enjoy their music.
    What's my secret consequence?

    I feel like I am a fake.

16. I try to turn my friends on to lyrics about acceptance.
    They still prefer lyrics that put people down.
    What's my secret reward?

    I think about finding different friends.

17. People say I'm the life of the party.
    I continually crack jokes.
    What's my secret consequence?

    I'm afraid to show my serious side.

18. I say "No" to hanging out with friends because I need time alone.
    They are angry with me.
    What's my secret reward?

    I take care of my needs.

(Continued on the next page)

I've Got a Secret *(Continued)*

19. I am pressured to pursue a career that pleases my family.
    I am accepted into their preferred school.
    What's my secret consequence?
    I'm not being true to myself or truthful to my family.

20. My interests and abilities point me to a specific career.
    People put down my aspirations.
    What's my secret reward?
    I have faith in myself.

21. I love to stay constantly connected to my friends.
    I turn off my phone during a family activity.
    What's my secret reward?
    I respect the people who are present.

22. I'm available 24/7 by cell phone.
    People need me 24/7.
    What's my secret consequence?
    I sacrifice my privacy and time.

23. I tell lots of people about how I was wronged and by whom.
    It feels good to get it off my chest.
    What's my secret consequence?
    I hurt someone else's reputation.

24. I plan to marry someone my friends and family approve of.
    The person is wonderful but I am not in love.
    What's my secret consequence?
    I am not doing right by myself or the person I plan to marry.

25. I am madly in love with someone who abuses me.
    I tell myself that the good times outweigh the bad.
    What's my secret consequence?
    I am fooling myself.

26. I have a problem.
    Drugs and alcohol help me forget temporarily.
    What's my secret consequence?
    I eventually have to face the problem.

27. I seek counseling for a problem.
    Some people make fun of me.
    What's my secret reward?
    I am helping myself.

28. I stand up for a cause I believe in.
    Some friends abandon me.
    What's my secret reward?
    I find out who my real friends are.

TEENS – ACTIONS, CONSEQUENCES, REWARDS

I've Got a Secret

FOR THE FACILITATOR

I. Purpose
To differentiate between apparent and actual consequences and rewards.

II. Skills
Identify fifteen genuine consequences from actions that gain superficial rewards.
Identify thirteen genuine rewards from actions that appear to result in negative outcomes.
Compose one or more teen scenarios for peers to consider.
Analyze at least one peer-composed scenario and state what to do.
Identify the overt and covert consequences and rewards of decisions.

III. Possible Activities
a. Ask for a volunteer to play Game Show Host.
b. Instruct the host to write "I've Got a Secret" on the board.
c. Give the I've Got a Secret handout to the host. Review the Game Show Host Instructions with the person.
d. Explain: "There are no right or wrong responses. Contestants may ask for help from others in the room."
e. The host reads the questions as contestants take turns responding.
f. The italicized text is read only after a contestant responds and is another suggestion, not the only answer.
g. After the game, distribute the handout to all participants.
h. Encourage teens to identify additional secret consequences and rewards in each scenario.

IV. Enrichment Activities
a. Distribute strips of paper.
b. Ask teens to anonymously compose at least one scenario in which a teen must make a decision.
c. Place strips of paper face down at the front of the room.
d. In each turn, teens do the following:
   - Go to the front of the room and read a scenario aloud.
   - State what one would do.
   - Identify the apparent or superficial consequences or rewards.
   - Identify the actual or deeper consequences or rewards.
   - Receive peer feedback.

DANGERS 4

The world is not dangerous because of those who do harm but because of those who look at it without doing anything.
~ Albert Einstein

Addiction Feud .... page 51 ▶
Teens discuss substance addiction and apply the concepts to other addictions.

Recovery Choices .... page 53 ▶
Teens identify risk factors, choices, treatment options, and research resources.

Teenage Undercover Peace Agent .... page 55 ▶
Teens find alternatives for physical fighting and create non-violence messages.

FOOD GLORIOUS FOOD – OR IS IT? .... page 57 ▶
Teens identify emotional aspects, body image, and other food issues.

Vehicle Vows .... page 59 ▶
Teens create messages about the dangers of unsafe driving and the rewards of safety.

SEXUAL SITUATIONS – WHAT COULD HAPPEN? .... page 63 ▶
Teens identify the emotional and social consequences of sexual issues.

Self-Harm Help .... page 65 ▶
Teens practice coping skills and describe personal power pledges.

Contemplate My Life .... page 69 ▶
Teens share capacities to overcome and become greater than their suffering.

Gang Busters .... page 71 ▶
Teens identify safe exit plans, new self-images and support resources.

GUN SAFETY PYRAMID .... page 73 ▶
Teens complete a gun safety word puzzle and debate gun-related controversies.

Dating Violence Prevention .... page 75 ▶
Teens develop a policy for sports players to prevent dating violence and abuse.

Break the Bullying Cycle .... page 77 ▶
Teens describe bullying cycles, roles, and ways to break the cycle.

REMINDER:
Save completed handouts in "My Actions Book" (see pages 11-14)

Chapter 4 - Dangers Behavioral Coping Skills

Throughout the chapter, teens will communicate through oral, written and creative expression and give and receive feedback.

Teens: Skills in each activity.
Facilitators: Competencies to evaluate.

Addiction Feud
- Explain six concepts regarding addiction and recovery.

Recovery Choices
- Identify risk factors when there is a choice to act in favor of prevention or recovery.

Teenage Undercover Peace Agent
- Describe motives, risks, behaviors, and plans to prevent campus violence.

Food Glorious Food – or is it?
- Specify ways starving, binging, purging and other actions affect body, emotions, and social life.

Vehicle Vows
- Demonstrate three or more safe driving rules through a variety of creative expression techniques.

Sexual Situations – What Could Happen?
- Write responses to twelve questions about emotional aspects of premature sex versus abstaining.

Self-Harm Help
- Identify causes, the falsity of the fix, and five or more healthy alternatives to self-harm.

Contemplate My Life
- Personalize reasons to choose life and state ways to make the most of capabilities.

Gang Busters
- Give reasons people join gangs, the percieved benefits, why and how to leave, and ways to reinvent an image.

Gun Safety Pyramid
- State five or more gun safety concepts. Discuss and debate five weapon-related controversies.

Dating Violence Prevention
- Define and discuss types of abuse, positive behavioral expectations, policies, and resources.

Break the Bullying Cycle
- Describe the role of the person who bullies, the person who is bullied, and the bystander – and three ways to break the cycle.

Dangers

Addiction Feud

Team Name: _____	Team Name: _____
Definition Key Words	Definition Key Words
Role of Dopamine	Role of Dopamine
Risk Factors	Risk Factors
Consequences	Consequences
Treatment	Treatment
Recovery Rewards	Recovery Rewards

TEENS – ACTIONS, CONSEQUENCES, REWARDS

Addiction Feud

FOR THE FACILITATOR

I. Purpose
To share information about teen addiction, consequences, and the rewards of recovery with peers.

II. Skills
State facts about substance addiction and other addictions.

III. Possible Activities
a. Tell teens there used to be a television spot which showed an egg on the sidewalk, fried by the sun, and compared it to a brain, "fried" on drugs.
b. Encourage a discussion of the special effects of substances on teen brains.
   Possibilities
   - Risk-taking, decision-making, and poor judgment.
   - Later addiction especially when combined with mood and stress issues.
   - Mood swings, panic attacks, paranoia, etc.
c. Divide teens into two teams; teammates sit together to collaborate.
d. Each team chooses its name and elects a captain to note their ideas.
e. Distribute the *Addiction Feud* handout to each team.
f. Allow about fifteen minutes for each team to research the categories.
g. The group re-convenes and a volunteer Addition Feud Host copies the handout outline onto the board. Team captains to alternately list brief responses on the board.
h. The group discusses the information.
   Concepts to elicit if not covered by the teams:

Definition of Substance Addiction
Psychological and/or physical dependence; craving, seeking, using despite consequences; a disease.
Role of Dopamine
Brain chemical that affects feelings of pleasure. Eventually, more of the substance is required to feel high, then just to feel normal, and then to avoid pain.
Risk Factors
Family history, emotional issues, abuse, peer pressure, role models, media and personal choices.
Consequences
Health problems, dangerous driving and risky behavior, accidents e.g., swimming, boating; problems with school, sports, friends, family and dating; unplanned and/or unsafe sex; violence and crimes; suicides.
Treatment
Medication, therapy, coping skills, family counseling, clean and sober friends, and activities.
Recovery Rewards
Physical and mental wellness; peak performance, healthier relationships, handling challenges and productive pursuits.

IV. Enrichment Activities
a. Encourage a discussion about different types of addictions, e.g., food, gambling, pornography, etc.
b. Provide future opportunities for teens to create *Addiction Feud* games regarding other topics.
c. Follow-up with the *Recovery Choices* handout, page 53, to prompt teens to personalize addiction concepts.

Dangers

Recovery Choices

1. **Check the boxes in front of your issues regarding alcohol and drug addiction potential.**
   - ☐ Family members with substance abuse or addiction problems. _____
   - ☐ Unknown family history. _____
   - ☐ Substance abuse by people in my early childhood home. _____
   - ☐ Family history of unwanted thoughts, feelings and actions issues. _____
   - ☐ Substance abuse by people in my present home. _____
   - ☐ My own use of substances. _____
   - ☐ My own unwanted thoughts, feelings and actions issues. _____
   - ☐ Any type of abuse in my past or present. _____
   - ☐ High stress in my past or present. _____
   - ☐ Peer pressure to drink or use substances. _____
   - ☐ Role models who drink or use substances. _____
   - ☐ Media messages that glamorize alcohol and drugs. _____
   - ☐ Friends who use alcohol or drugs. _____
   - ☐ Attendance at parties and places where people are drinking and using substances. _____
   - ☐ My own issues with conduct, defiance, rebelliousness. _____
   - ☐ My own issues with learning. _____
   - ☐ My own issues with paying attention and/or hyperactivity. _____
   - ☐ Problems I would like to avoid or forget. _____
   - ☐ Boredom. _____
   - ☐ Cravings for substances. _____
   - ☐ Constant thoughts about obtaining and using substances. _____
   - ☐ Continued use despite negative consequences. (school problems, arrests, etc.) _____
   - ☐ Withdrawal when I do not have the substance. (hangovers, crashing, etc.) _____
   - ☐ Need more and more of the substance for the same effects, _____
   - ☐ No longer able to achieve pleasure from the substance. _____
   - ☐ Use of the substance to feel normal or avoid withdrawal. _____
   - ☐ Loss of interest in or pleasure from other activities. _____
2. **Place a "C" on the line after each item above in which you have any sort of choice(s).**
3. **Consider your risk factors, signs of addiction and choices. What will you do?**
   - ☐ Give in to my genetics. (I cannot help my family history.)
   - ☐ Blame my environment. (I cannot change people, places, and the media.)
   - ☐ Believe I am ruined because of past or present abuse.
   - ☐ Decide I will not experiment with alcohol and drugs.
   - ☐ Seek help if I have substance-related problems.
   - ☐ Seek help for substance-related or other family issues.
   - ☐ Seek help for unwanted thoughts, feelings and actions issues.
   - ☐ Learn coping and problem solving skills to deal with abuse, stress and other past or present issues.
   - ☐ Help others with substance-related issues.
   - ☐ Learn healthy ways to handle life's challenges.
   - ☐ Choose clean and sober friends, parties and activities.
   - ☐ Choose songs, movies, videos, and role models that promote a clean and sober lifestyle.
   - ☐ Engage in healthy activities I enjoy or used to enjoy.
   - ☐ Find and pursue my passion and experience a natural high.
4. **What will you do first?**

_____

_____

TEENS – ACTIONS, CONSEQUENCES, REWARDS

Recovery Choices

FOR THE FACILITATOR

I. Purpose
To distinguish substance-related issues over which one does and does not have choice(s). Ideally this session will follow the *Addiction Feud* session, page 51, in which teens identified generic factors that they will now personalize.

II. Skills
Identify risk factors and signs of addictions.
Select the correct twenty-three from among twenty-seven factors over which teens have choice(s).
Select at least five and up to ten options to prevent or recover from substance-related issues.
Select options that demonstrate awareness of a teen's choices:
   Cannot choose family history or early childhood environmental exposure.
   Can choose to seek help for past or present issues e.g., abuse, trauma, family problems, etc.
   Can choose a clean and sober lifestyle, e.g., choices of friends and media messages to adopt.

III. Possible Activities
   a. Ask for a volunteer to draw on the board; whisper instructions to draw a brick or block with a piece chipped off and to point to the chip; ask teens what is depicted.
   b. Prompt teens to recall a related expression - *A chip off the old block*.
   c. Tell teens to guess its meaning (one is similar to one's parent or older family member).
   d. Encourage teens to share ways they do and do not resemble family members.
   e. Explain that addiction and substance-related issues may be linked to genetic and/or other factors.
   f. Distribute the *Recovery Choices* handout and review the instructions numbered 1-4 with the teens.
   g. Allow time for completion.
   h. Encourage teens to share responses within their comfort zones.
   i. Emphasize confidentiality "What is said in the room stays in the room."
      Answer Key
         Number 1 – individual responses.
         Number 2 – **only the first four items describe issues in which teens have no choices;** they *can* choose to seek help for past or current abuse, family and all other issues and symptoms.
         Number 3 – **only the first three items are not to be checked;** other choices depend on each teen's individual situations. All teens, even those without addiction or emotional issues, need to select the last five items.
         Number 4 – individual responses.

IV. Enrichment Activities
Encourage teens individually, in dyads or teams to research and share their results regarding the following issues:
   • Types of treatment (medical detoxification, sober living homes, individual and/or group counseling, twelve-step and other support groups, faith-based programs, etc.)
   • Insurance (required for some programs but not for others)
   • Costs (expensive to free)
   • Excuses – no insurance, cannot afford it, (untrue!); stigma (not really in view of the number of celebrities who go to rehabilitation programs and famous persons with addiction problems).
   • Reliable sources of further information, teen questions and answers, etc.
      Possibilities
         National Institute on Drug Abuse for Teens (NIDA)
         Substance Abuse and Mental Health Services Administration (SAMHSA)
         National Substance Abuse Index; also state and local government sites
         National Alliance for Mentally Ill (NAMI)

Teenage Undercover Peace Agent

Place the letters for the correct responses from the Facts Repository
onto the Undercover Log blanks.

FACTS REPOSITORY	
A. Weapons **B.** Unsafe sex **C.** Insults and disrespect **D.** Suicide attempts **E.** Anger management training **F.** Being hit, shoved or bumped **G.** Realize walking away is better than an arrest **H.** An ongoing disagreement **I.** Conflict resolution **J.** Never carry weapons **K.** Poor anger control **L.** Avoid being alone if threatened **M.** An audience who encouraged the fight **N.** Talk to a trusted adult	**O.** Safe way to report threats, weapons, gangs **P.** Not wanting to look like a loser **Q.** Younger children and be a positive role model **R.** Substances **S.** Dating issues **T.** Take time-out **U.** Peer assistance leadership program **V.** Wanting to get or keep a tough reputation **W.** Understanding and acceptance of differences **X.** Loving to fight **Y.** Consider the consequences of violence **Z.** Never fight someone who has a weapon

Undercover Log

Today I am on the high school beat and detected these motives for physical fights: _____, _____, _____, _____, _____, _____, _____, _____, _____.

Disturbances were more likely to cause serious bodily injury if perps were carrying _____ or using _____.

Perps who fought were more likely to engage in risky behaviors like _____ or _____.

I confidentially mentioned these solutions to the individuals that seemed most troubled: _____, _____, _____, _____, _____, _____, _____, _____, _____.

My plans to prevent violence on campus:

Collaborate with students to design a _____, start a _____, volunteer to mentor _____, and work with students to increase their _____.

TEENS – ACTIONS, CONSEQUENCES, REWARDS

Teenage Undercover Peace Agent

FOR THE FACILITATOR

I. Purpose
To identify motives, consequences, and solutions for physical fighting and work toward its prevention.

II. Skills
Demonstrate knowledge about physical fighting by completing a mock Undercover Log noting the following:
  Nine motives
  Two risks for bodily injury
  Two associated risky behaviors
  Nine solutions
  Four plans to prevent violence on campus
Actively engage in efforts to prevent physical fighting via creation of posters, poems, slogans, etc.

III. Possible Activities
   a. Ask teens what they know about undercover agents (pose as someone else to gain trust and detect information).
   b. Explain that teens will assume the identity of a teen undercover peace agent.
   c. Distribute the *Teenage Undercover Peace Agent* handout; a volunteer reads the directions aloud.
   d. Allow time for completion.
   e. Encourage teens to share their responses.
      Possibilities
      - Motives – C, F, H, K, M, P, S, V, X
      - Bodily injury – A, R
      - Risky behaviors – B, D
      - Solutions – E, G, I, J, L, N, T, Y, Z
      - Plans to prevent violence on campus – O, U, Q, W

IV. Enrichment Activities
   a. Ask teens to share knowledge about conflict resolution and/or their experiences.
      Possibilities
      - Active listening
      - Sharing thoughts and feelings
      - Brainstorming solutions
      - Seeking compromises, win-win outcomes
   b. Encourage participants to create violence prevention messages and share them with teens in other classes, schools or groups.
      Possibilities
      - Posters
      - Essays
      - Bumper stickers, tee shirts, refrigerator magnet slogans
      - Poems
      - Song lyrics
      - Role plays or skits
      - School newspaper articles
      - Posts and blogs
      - Websites

Dangers ▶

Food Glorious Food – or is it?

1. What does milk mean to an infant?	2. What happens when children are rewarded with food?	3. How are food issues more complicated than giving up substances?	4. How are people affected by celebrity body images?	5. What's the problem with following a celebrity's diet?
6. What happens when one is on a so-called "diet"?	7. What happens when food becomes way too important?	8. How does obsessing about one's body image affect thoughts about food?	9. How does starving affect the body?	10. How does starving affect thoughts?
11. How does starving affect emotions?	12. How does food binging affect the body?	13. How does food binging affect thoughts?	14. How does food binging affect emotions?	15. What's a better and healthier word or phrase for "diet"?
16. What's helpful about the term "eating plan"?	17. What emotions cause some people to turn to food for comfort?	18. Instead of food, to whom or what can people turn for comfort?	19. How does exercise affect the body?	20. How does exercise affect thoughts?
21. How does exercise affect emotions?	22. How does guilt about overeating affect a person?	23. What are some signs that someone has a problem with food?	24. How could a person with food issues get help?	25. What's the problem with constantly turning to food for comfort?
26. How does purging affect emotions?	27. How does purging affect the body?	28. What's the problem with too much exercise?	29. What's the problem with drugs that supposedly increase strength?	30. How do eating disorders affect thoughts?
31. What is meant by a person's "natural body build"?	32. What can happen when one tries to change one's natural body build?	33. What happens when a person goes to body image extremes to please a partner?	34. What happens when people keep eating problems a secret?	35. It is said that an eating disorder is "not about the food." What is it about?

TEENS – ACTIONS, CONSEQUENCES, REWARDS

Food Glorious Food – or is it?

FOR THE FACILITATOR

I. Purpose
To identify food-related issues, actions, consequences, and ways to cope.

II. Skills
Identify how starving, binging, and purging affects body, mind, and emotions.
Share four ideas about food related to love, rewards, comfort, and healthier alternatives.
Describe three social aspects related to body image and food extremes.
Explain twelve concepts about the emotional aspects of food extremes.
Discuss seven statements related to exercise and natural body build.
Brainstorm ways that food issues could affect own life.

III. Possible Activities
   a. Before the session, photocopy the *Food Glorious Food … or is it?* handout and cut out the boxes.
   b. Place the cutouts face down at the front of the room.
   c. At the start of the session write *Food Glorious Food … or is it?* on the board; ask for a vote. *Is food always glorious or is it not?*
   d. Explain that people sometimes turn to food as comfort as if it were a drug or a solution.
   e. Explain that teens will take turns sharing ideas about food and body image.
   f. In each turn teens go to the front of the room, pick up a cutout and read it aloud, and volunteers respond.

   Some concepts to elicit if not covered by the teens:
   1. Love, nurturing; needs being met
   2. Food becomes emotionally linked
   3. Cannot give up food entirely
   4. Try to achieve their bodies
   5. May not be appropriate or safe
   6. Obsessed with restricting foods
   7. Turn to it for emotional needs
   8. Obsess about "forbidden" foods
   9. Head and stomach aches; low energy
   10. Focus constantly on food and weight
   11. May be depressed, anxious, isolative
   12. Weight issues and empty calories
   13. Obsess about food and lack of control
   14. Possible guilt, self-loathing, shame
   15. Food plan
   16. Focuses on healthy food choices
   17. Loneliness, fear, sadness, anxiety
   18. Trusted adult, exercise
   19. Burns calories, tones muscles
   20. May help clarity and energy
   21. Lifts mood, decreases anxiety
   22. Eat more to numb the guilt
   23. Weight and mood changes, secrecy
   24. Talk with nurse, counselor, or M.D.
   25. Temporary and ignores real issues
   26. Depression, shame, low esteem
   27. Stomach and other health problems
   28. Becomes an obsession, stop doing other things
   29. Side effects harm body and mind
   30. Obsess about food and body image issues
   31. Genetics re: bone structure, weight
   32. An uphill battle, may not win
   33. Won't last. Not unconditional love
   34. They avoid or delay getting help
   35. Emotional, social and physical issues

IV. Enrichment Activities
   a. Encourage teens to share their favorite food-related family traditions, ethnic foods, holiday fare, etc.
   b. Ask teens to brainstorm ways that eating issues could affect one's family and social life.
      Possibilities
      • Avoid parties, holiday dinners, graduations, weddings, maybe even movies (buttered popcorn).
      • Plan ways to keep an eating disorder a secret.
      • Hide weight gains or losses under bulky clothes.
      • Feel embarrassed because of eating very rapidly and/or overeating.
      • Obsess about taking home all the leftovers.
      • Try to eat without being bothered with conversation.
   c. Ask teens for tips on how to eat healthy. Request for a volunteer to list the tips. Distribute the list to teens.

Dangers ▶

Vehicle Vows
Drive to Dance

Warm-Up

Pick a rhyme and make up dance steps or cheer-leading routines and then perform the lyrics and movements.

Don't drink, drug or text when you drive If you want to stay alive.	Cell phone talk and passenger chatter Can be a life or death matter.
In the car - no food and drink. Use your brain - stop and think.	Paralysis, pain, death and sorrow Could ruin your own and others' tomorrows.

Main Attraction

**Make up lyrics and accompanying dance steps or cheer routines about safe driving.
Practice with your team and then perform for your fans.
Use the space below to compose and choreograph.**

Vehicle Vows Passenger Plight

Warm-Up

Perform the scenario below.

2 Cast Members: Driver and Passenger

Driver: "We're going to have a great night driving around."
Passenger: "Okay."
Driver, while driving: "I'm going to text Alan to tell him we'll pick him up."
Passenger asks audience: "What would you do?"

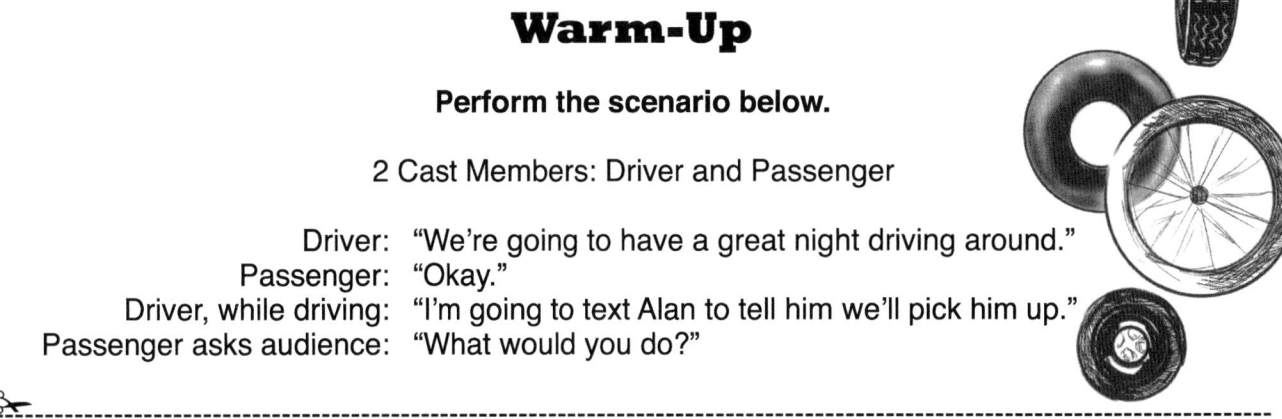

Main Attraction

Write and rehearse a screenplay about a passenger in
potential danger who must make a decision.
After a couple of lines, the passenger asks the audience what they would do.
Use the script outline below. (It is not necessary to use all the lines)

Number of Cast Members _____

Names of Cast Members

_____: " _____ "

_____: " _____ "

_____: " _____ "

_____: " _____ "

_____: " _____ "

Passenger: "What would you do?"

_____

_____

_____

_____

_____

_____

Vehicle Vows
Post or Poster?

Create a safe driving poster using drawings, doodles, symbols, squiggles, collages, cartoons, caricatures, or any other visuals. Add words if you wish.
or…
Compose an essay/post giving safe driving tips to teens in a friendly, funny, dramatic, or other way.
or …
Do both!!!

TEENS – ACTIONS, CONSEQUENCES, REWARDS

Vehicle Vows

FOR THE FACILITATOR

I. Purpose
To create messages that convey the rewards of safe driving and the consequences of unsafe driving.

II. Skills
Compose, choreograph, perform, and observe dance or cheer-leading routines about driving hazards.
Write, enact and view scenarios about a passenger who decides ways to avoid danger.
Depict and/or describe safe driving through posters, essays, or posts.
Incorporate at least three safe-driving concepts from the list of *Possibilities* below or related ideas.

III. Possible Activities
a. The *Vehicle Vows* handouts are to be presented in three sessions.
b. At the start of each session, teens brainstorm safety concepts as a volunteer lists ideas on the board.
   Possibilities
   - Do not drive under the influence of alcohol or drugs.
   - Avoid distractions – phone, texts, joking with passengers, shouting to other drivers, eating, etc.
   - Never drive when sad, crying, preoccupied with a problem, angry, anxious, drowsy, etc.
   - Be careful when excited – this could make a person feel invincible.
   - Avoid racing and other reckless behavior.
   - Prevent personal road rage. Do not react to others' road rage.
   - Wear seatbelts in cars and trucks; helmets on motorcycles and bikes.
c. At the start of each session introduce the activity and proceed as follows:
   Drive to Dance – Before the session, photocopy the handout and cut the 4 boxes on the broken lines.
   Recruit volunteers for the Warm-Up and provide them with the cutout rhyme.
   The Warm-Up teams briefly practice the rhyme and movements a distance from peers.
   At the start of the session, the Warm-Up teams read the rhyme in unison and perform.
   Distribute the Main Attraction cutout to all participants.
   Divide into a workable number of teams. Warm-Up team members join Main Attraction teams.
   Teams compose, choreograph, rehearse and perform for peers who applaud and provide feedback.
   Passenger Plight – Before the session, photocopy the handout and cut on the broken lines.
   Recruit two volunteers for the Warm-Up team and provide them with the cutout scenario.
   The Warm-Up team briefly rehearses the scenario a distance from peers.
   At the start of the session, Warm-Up team performs the scenario.
   The actor portraying the passenger asks the audience "What would you do?" and elicits solutions.
   Distribute the Main Attraction cutout to all participants.
   They may complete it individually or enact scenes in teams as below.
   Divide into casts of two to four actors. Warm-Up members join the Main Attraction teams.
   Teams write, rehearse, and perform plays, and the passengers elicit responses to "What would you do?"
   Post or Poster? – Before the session, photocopy the handout and have color markers available.
   A volunteer reads the directions aloud; allow time for completion.
   Encourage teens to share their posters, essays or posts and to receive peer feedback.

IV. Enrichment Activities
a. Enable teens to perform routines and skits for other classes, schools or groups and to display posters.
b. Suggest that teens research the main causes of injury and death among young people, report to peers and initiate a campaign about safety: assemblies, discussions and debates; speakers and/or information from highway patrol, SADD (Students Against Destructive Decisions), and other organizations to create school websites and find ways to spread the safety message.

Dangers

SEXUAL SITUATIONS – WHAT COULD HAPPEN?

Fill in the blanks with your opinions.
Your responses are private unless you decide to share.

Action	What Could Happen?	How Would You Feel About Each Outcome?
You sext a nude photo of yourself.	1. 2.	1. 2.
You have unprotected sex.	3. 4.	3. 4.
You and your partner disagree about whether to have sex.	5. 6.	5. 6.
You and your partner disagree about a pregnancy.	7. 8.	7. 8.
You have safe sex.	9. 10.	9. 10.
You decide to wait.	11. 12.	11. 12.

TEENS – ACTIONS, CONSEQUENCES, REWARDS

SEXUAL SITUATIONS – WHAT COULD HAPPEN?

FOR THE FACILITATOR

I. Purpose
To identify possible outcomes of sexual situations.

II. Skills
Identify two possible outcomes and how a person would feel about each of the following:
Sexting a nude photo
Having unprotected sex.
Disagreeing about whether to have sex.
Disagreeing about a pregnancy.
Having safe sex.
Deciding to wait.

III. Possible Activities
  a. Explain that the situations encourage teens to think about them, write their opinions, and decide whether to share.
  b. Distribute the *Sexual Situations – What Could Happen?* handout.
  c. Allow time for completion.
  d. Encourage teens who are willing to share their responses and receive peer feedback.

Possibilities

Action	What Could Happen?	How Would You Feel About Each Outcome?
You sext a nude photo of yourself.	1. The person could send it to *everyone*. 2. People who you don't want to know about it, could find out.	1. Embarrassed or violated or some teens may be ok with it. 2. Upset if parents or caregivers find out.
You have unprotected sex.	3. Pregnancy. 4. Sexually Transmitted Disease.	3. Upset or glad about pregnancy. 4. Scared about the illness.
You and your partner disagree about whether to have sex.	5. Arguments 6. Show affection in other ways.	5. Anxious due to conflict. 6. Okay with a compromise.
You and your partner disagree about a pregnancy.	7. An unwanted abortion or an unplanned baby. 8. The relationship may suffer due to the conflict.	7. Upset because one partner is against the decision. 8. Sad if the relationship ends over the issue.
You have safe sex.	9. No pregnancy or disease. 10. The relationship could heat up / cool down.	9. Relieved due to prevention. 10. Upset to have given in to having sex if the relationship ends.
You decide to wait.	11. Your partner could agree or break up. 12. You would know if your partner truly cares for you.	11. Great if partner agrees or disappointment with a break up. 12. Glad that the truth about the partner was revealed.

Note: *Some teens may imagine only positive outcomes for sexual activities and negative outcomes for abstaining. Some teens may feel the opposite. Encourage respectful discussion among those willing to disclose.*

IV. Enrichment Activities
  a. Encourage teens to anonymously write questions they have about sex on slips of paper.
  b. Place them in a container.
  c. Arrange in advance for the school nurse or a public health professional to visit and respond to the questions.

Self-Harm Help – Emoticon

E-mo-ti-con = a combination of emotion and icon -
a group of keyboard characters that are used to represent a facial expression,
such as a smile :-) = ☺ or a frown :-(= ☹

What are the bandages covering up?

_____

Some people cut, burn or harm their bodies because of painful emotions.
Label each bandage with feelings teens may have.

In what ways could self-harm deceive by seeming to help?

_____
_____
_____
_____

TEENS – ACTIONS, CONSEQUENCES, REWARDS

Self-Harm Help – Alternatives

Describe how you can change destructive or other unwanted behavior.

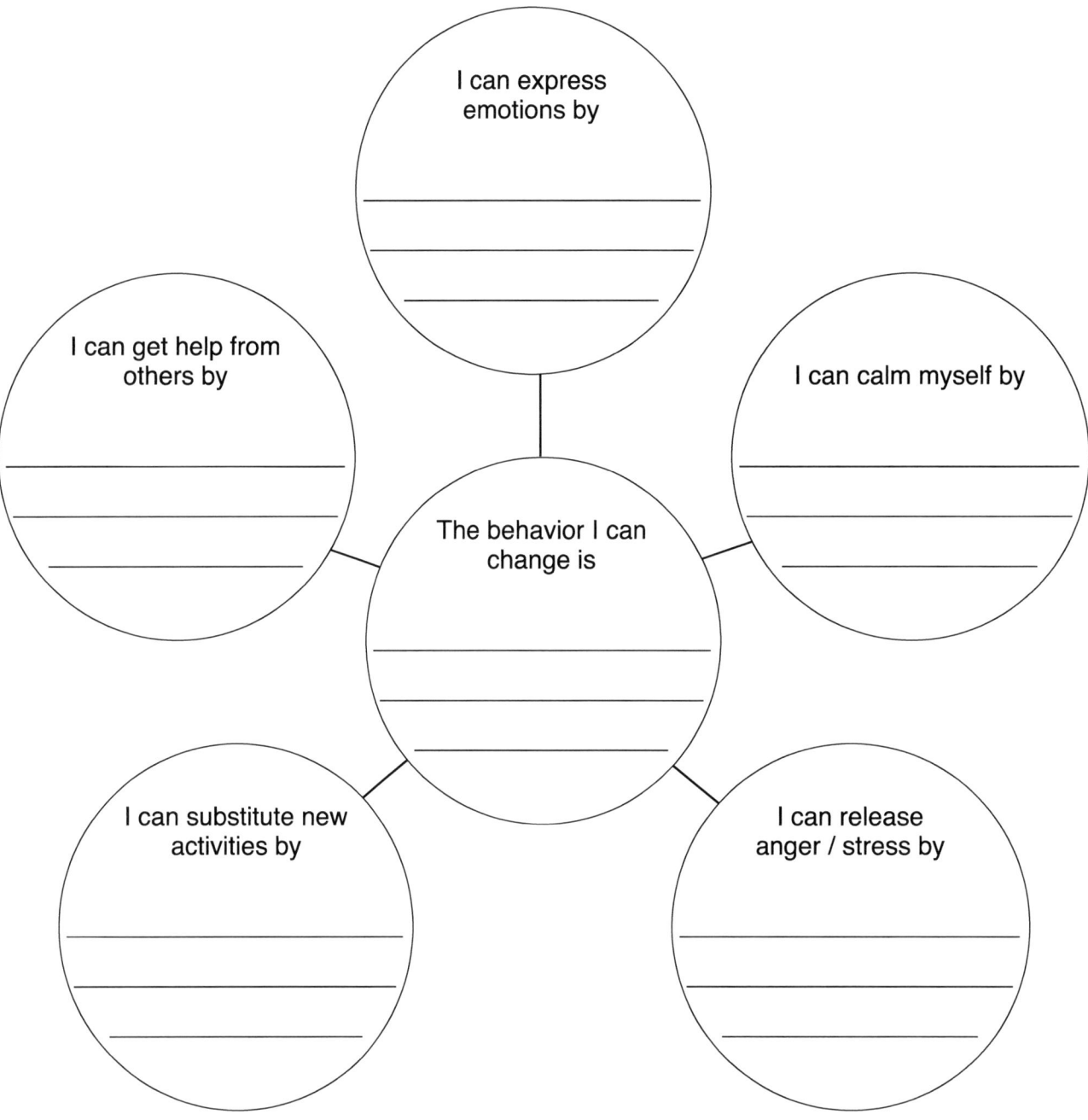

In what other ways can you handle your feelings and your life?

_____
_____
_____

Dangers ▶

Self-Harm Help – Positive Personal Power

People who feel powerless often do anything to think they control *something*.
Example: "I have control over when, where and how I cut myself" (or other harmful action).
Real Control
Acknowledge your thoughts, feelings and actions.
Uphold or change them to promote POSITIVE personal power.

My Positive Personal Power Pledge

I choose to…

Think _____

Feel _____

Act _____

Change _____

Accept _____

Forgive _____

Say "No" to _____

Say "Yes" to _____

Stand up to _____

Believe in this power beyond myself _____

My Five Favorite Power Words and/or Symbols

TEENS – ACTIONS, CONSEQUENCES, REWARDS

Self-Harm Help

FOR THE FACILITATOR

I. **Purpose**
To identify causes, the falsity of the *fix* and healthy alternatives for self harm or other unwanted behavior; to empower oneself and represent power concepts through verbal and/or non-verbal cues.

II. **Skills**
Describe six feelings that underlie self-harm and four ways that self-harm falsely seems to help.
Define a behavior to change and note ways to perform five specific coping skills and add others.
Make a positive personal power pledge by elaborating on ten prompts.
Write and/or depict five favorite power words and/or symbols.

III. **Possible Activities**
   a. Ask for a volunteer to draw a muscular person lifting a heavy weight on the board.
   b. Ask the group "What idea is shown?" (strength, power).
   c. Suggest that some teens feel powerless and try to gain control in unusual ways.
   d. Distribute the three *Self-Harm Help* handouts, *Emoticons, Alternatives*, and *Positive Personal Power*.
   e. Direct teens to complete the pages in the above order, take their time, and ask for help as needed.
   f. Allow time for completion.
   g. Encourage teens to share their responses and receive peer feedback.
   Possibilities
   Emoticon – **The bandages cover up** a person who has feelings.
   - Feelings teens may have – shyness, self-hatred, emptiness, emotionally void, anger, powerlessness, guilt, etc.
   - Self harm seems to help because emotional pain is transferred to physical pain, or deadness/numbness is transformed into feeling something; people may want to punish themselves; endorphins are released and teens may feel a release of tension or a "high"; they may want to fit in with peers who self-mutilate.

   Emphasize that any of the seemingly quick fixes are temporary and prevent teens from finding healthy alternatives to cope with emotions and life.

   Alternatives – The behavior to change – Individual responses.
   - **Express emotions** – Talk with a trusted adult; paint, draw, scribble; journal, compose a poem or song, or write negative feelings on paper and then tear it up; listen to music that expresses the emotions one is experiencing.
   - **Calm oneself** – Take a hot bath or shower; cuddle a pet; wrap up in a warm blanket; massage one's neck, hands and feet; listen to music that soothes the person; use aroma therapy.
   - **Release anger/stress** – Exercise vigorously; punch or scream into a pillow; squeeze a stress ball or clay; write an angry letter and then tear it up; rip magazines; play an instrument, shout (if alone where no one else can hear), sing; forgive.
   - **Substitute activities** – Healthy substitutes are socializing, writing, reading, exercising, volunteering, drawing, etc. *(The following substitute activities may be shared based on the facilitator's beliefs and the maturity and needs of participants; these methods are merely quick fixes, not coping skills, but may appeal to teens who need immediate substitution for impulsive self mutilation – write on skin with a red felt-tipped pen instead of cutting; rub ice on the skin or snap a rubber band on one's wrist).*
   - **Get help** – Tell a trusted adult; research reliable resources; seek therapy.
   - **In what other ways** – Individual responses.

   Positive Personal Power – Individual responses; emphasize choices, using one's voice, etc.

IV. **Enrichment Activities**
   a. Encourage teens to research ancient, ethnic, religious, spiritual, and modern symbols of power.
   b. Challenge teens to paint rocks, place power words and symbols on a mural or bulletin board.

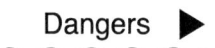 Dangers

Contemplate My Life

Personalize the quotations below with your responses.

The most authentic thing about us is our capacity to create, to overcome, to endure, to transform, to love, and to be greater than our suffering.
~ Ben Okri

I have the capacity …

to create

_____

to overcome (obstacles)

_____

to endure

_____

to transform

_____

to love

_____

to be greater than my suffering by

_____

To make yourself less than you can be is also a form of suicide.
~ Benjamin Lichtenberg

I will make myself all that I can be by …

_____

_____

_____

TEENS – ACTIONS, CONSEQUENCES, REWARDS

Contemplate My Life

FOR THE FACILITATOR

I. Purpose
To personalize reasons to identify ways to make the most of one's life and capabilities.

II. Skills
Describe at least one obstacle to overcome, situation to endure, trait or trouble to transform, entity to love, technique to be greater than suffering.
State three ways to be all one can be.
Compose six-word inspirational quotes after reading the two quotations.

III. Possible Activities
a. Ask teens to brainstorm possible emotions and situations that lead some people to think about suicide.
   Possibilities
   - Being Bullied
   - Crises
   - Guilt
   - Helplessness
   - Hopelessness
   - Loneliness / Isolation
   - Losses
   - Perceived failure
   - Pressures
   - Worthlessness

b. Emphasize that if a teen or peer is thinking or talking about harming self or others, they need to tell a trusted adult, go to a hospital emergency department, or call 911 or their emergency services number. Secrets *kill* if a person is a danger to self/others; to tell may save a life.

c. Distribute the *Contemplate My Life* handout; a volunteer reads the directions and quotations aloud.

d. Allow time for completion.

e. Encourage teens to share their responses and receive peer feedback.
   Possibilities
   I have the capacity to …
   - CREATE: positive qualities, hopes, dreams, goals, skills; pictures, poems, music, charities
   - OVERCOME (OBSTACLES): family, physical, emotional, financial; criticism, bullying, exclusion
   - ENDURE: change thinking about a situation; strengthen hope and faith
   - TRANSFORM: thoughts, feelings and actions; unhealthy habits into healthy ones
   - LOVE: life, oneself; people who love and respect in return; nature, art, music
   - BE GREATER THAN SUFFERING: by spirituality; volunteer, help others
   - MAKE MYSELF ALL THAT I CAN BE: by 100% effort in school, set goals and take baby steps daily toward the goals

IV. Enrichment Activities
a. Encourage teens to compose their own six-word inspirational quotes; write examples on the board:
   - *Fall seven times, stand up eight.* ~ Japanese Proverb
   - *Once you choose hope, anything's possible.* ~ Christopher Reeve
   - Prompt teens to read their quotations aloud and receive peer feedback.
   - Ask teens who are willing to submit quotes anonymously for photocopying and distribution to peers.
   - Suggest that teens to make their quotes into refrigerator magnets, post-it notes, posters, bumper stickers, etc.

b. Encourage teens to create "I am" statements. ("I am _____.")
   - "I am worth it."
   - "I am capable."

Ask them to put them all together in a poster.

Dangers

Gang Busters

Gang: people who share a common purpose usually involving criminal activity and violence.

Brainstorm with your teammates. Elect a secretary to list your ideas under your team's heading.

Team A	Team B	Team C	Team D	Team E
Why do people join a gang?	*What do people get out of being in a gang?*	*What are the reasons people want to leave a gang?*	*How can people leave a gang safely?*	*How can people reinvent their image and reputation?*
Ex: thrills	Ex: arrests	Ex: freedom	Ex: fade out	Ex: employee
1.	1.	1.	1.	1.
2.	2.	2.	2.	2.
3.	3.	3.	3.	3.
4.	4.	4.	4.	4.
5.	5.	5.	5.	5.
Additional Ideas:	Additional Ideas:	Additional Ideas:	Additional Ideas:	Additional Ideas:

TEENS – ACTIONS, CONSEQUENCES, REWARDS

Gang Busters

FOR THE FACILITATOR

I. Purpose
To identify the allure, consequences, reasons for leaving, safe exit plans and new self-images.

II. Skills
List at least five responses for each:
> Why do people join a gang?
> What do people get out of being in a gang?
> What are the reasons people want to leave a gang?
> How can people leave a gang safely?
> How can people reinvent their image and reputation?

III. Possible Activities
a. Ask teens for a definition of a gang and write their ideas on the board.
b. Distribute the *Gang Busters* handout. A volunteer reads the definition and directions aloud.
   Team Option
   • Divide teens into five teams; teams brainstorm. Each team's secretary records ideas under their headings.
   • Copy the handout outline onto the board.
   • The group re-convenes. Secretaries read aloud and list their teams' ideas on the board.
   Individual Option
   • Assign an equal number of teens to each heading(s) or allow teens choose a heading(s).
   • Teens write ideas independently under their heading(s) on their handouts.
   • Copy the handout outline onto the board.
   • Teens share their ideas; a volunteer lists them under the appropriate headings on the board.
   Possibilities

Team A	Team B	Team C	Team D	Team E
1. acceptance
2. protection
3. prestige
4. family tradition
5. money from drug sales, robberies	1. part of a group
2. tough reputation
3. thrills
4. popularity
5. family pride or tradition	1. victimization
2. substance abuse
3. poor grades
4. limited job options
5. probation	1. don't tell gang
2. tell trusted adult
3. be less available
4. excuses, curfews
5. gang interventionist	1. be responsible
2. no longer fear police
3. become a wage earner
4. get good grades
5. H.S. graduate, GED or college student

c. Validate that some gangs believe in "blood in, blood out" that one must be beaten-up or worse to leave; also some teens' family members may be in danger if teens try to leave.
d. People in danger need discreet help from law enforcement, gang interventionists, etc.
e. Encourage a discussion about the more common reasons people leave gangs – outgrow; partner disapproves; legal compliance e.g., no-contact orders or electronic monitoring; marriage, family and job responsibilities; involvement in social, recreational, faith-based activities, etc.

IV. Enrichment Activities
Prompt teens to explore the Office of Juvenile Justice and Delinquency Prevention Comprehensive Anti-Gang Initiative and other resources. Teams may research different aspects and report to the group.

GUN SAFETY PYRAMID

Use the clues and choices below to fill in the blank letters.

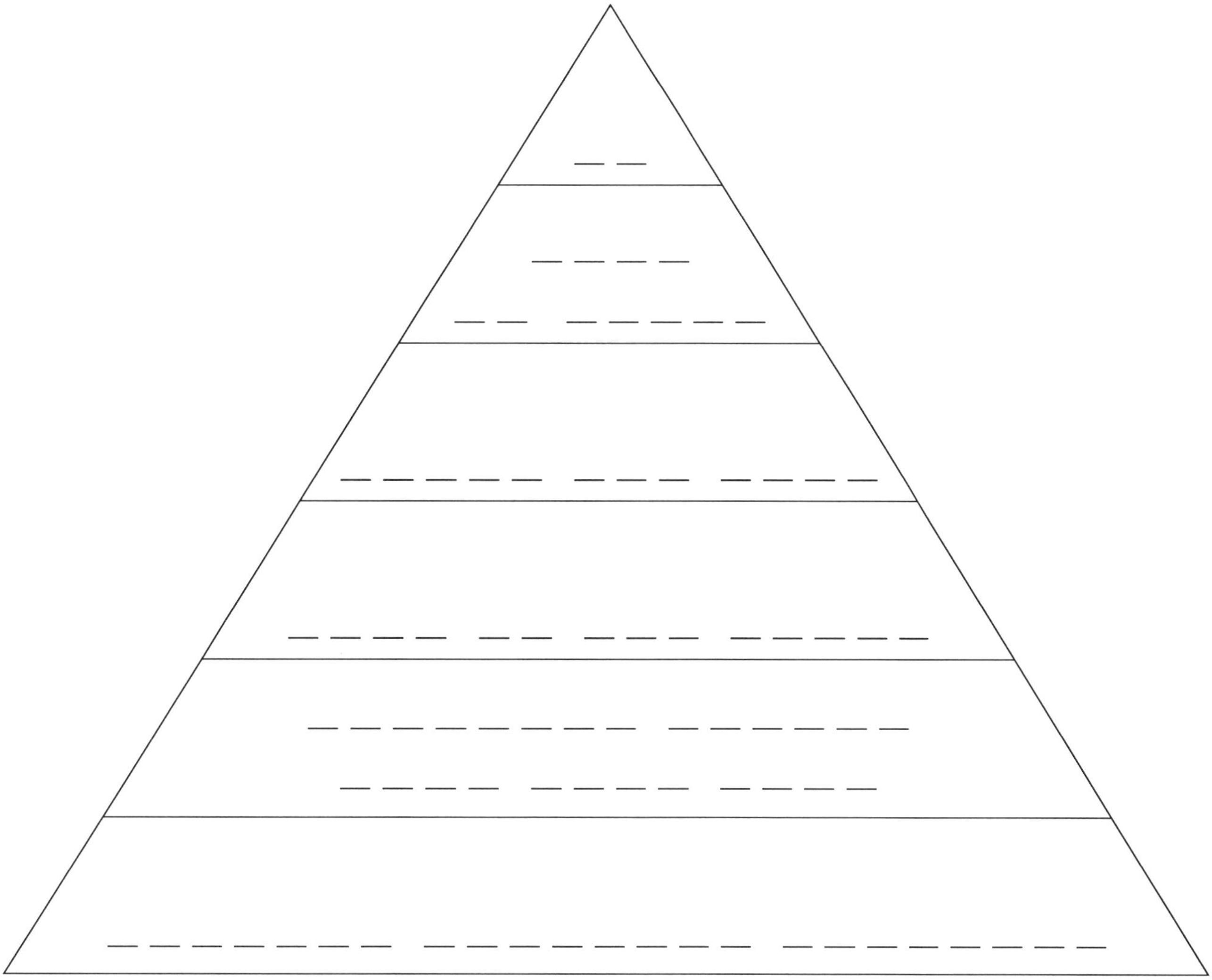

_ _

_ _ _

_ _ _ _ _

_ _ _ _ _ _ _ _

_ _ _ _ _ _ _ _ _ _ _ _

_ _ _ _ _ _ _ _ _ _ _ _ _ _ _

_ _

Clues from Top to Bottom Rows

ROW 1   What to say if someone offers to show you a gun.
ROWS 2, 3, 4   What to do if you see a gun.
ROW 5   The safest way to store guns.
ROW 6   People with guns for self-protection are more likely to be killed by the gun in these ways.

Choices in Random Order

Suicide, homicide, accident
No
Stop, do not touch
Unloaded, locked, away from ammo
Leave the area
Tell an adult

TEENS – ACTIONS, CONSEQUENCES, REWARDS

GUN SAFETY PYRAMID

FOR THE FACILITATOR

I. **Purpose**
To demonstrate awareness of gun safety concepts by completing a word puzzle; to consider both sides and formulate opinions about gun-related controversies.

II. **Skills**
State the correct safe reply when asked if one wants to see a gun.
Share three actions to take if an unsecured gun is observed.
Identify three ways a responsible adult gun owner can safely store a gun.
Note three ways people who have guns for self-protection are more likely to be killed by their guns.
Participate in debate(s), observe and comment on peers' debates about gun control, rights and issues.

III. **Possible Activities**
   a. Write "Guns – Why?" on the board.
   b. Ask "Why do people have guns?" (Hunting, self-protection, it's a right in most countries; to kill).
   c. Ask "Why are we talking about guns?" (Many teens are killed or injured by guns).
   d. Distribute the *Gun Safety Pyramid* handout; Point out the instructions and lists of clues and choices.
   e. Allow time for completion.
   f. Encourage teens to share their responses.
      Answer Key
      1. No
      2. Tell an adult
      3. Leave the area
      4. Stop, do not touch
      5. Unloaded, locked, away from ammo
      6. Suicide, homicide, accident
   g. Ask about some teens' reluctance to tell a parent/caregiver, teacher, etc. about someone havng a gun. Elicit that saving lives is more important than keeping a potentially deadly secret.

IV. **Enrichment Activities**
   a. Plan debates about gun control, rights and issues.
   b. List topics on the board and allow time for research of the second amendment or print out a copy for each of the teens.
      1. Should the second amendment "right to bear arms" be upheld or abolished? Why?
      2. Do background checks keep guns out of the hands of potentially dangerous criminals? Explain.
      3. Should teachers, counselors and principals be armed with guns? Explain.
      4. Does playing a shooter in video games make a teen more likely to shoot someone in real life? Explain.
      5. If more people own guns are we safer or at higher risk of injury or death?
   c. Allow individuals or teams to think about their points of view.
   d. Allow time for individuals or team members to prepare brief notes.
   e. Set a time limit for each side's arguments and rebuttals.
   f. Enforce rules – no interruptions and no audience comments or applause until after all debates are finished.
   g. Suggest that all debaters or team members are winners for taking a stand for their beliefs.
   h. Encourage applause for all debaters, elicit audience comments, e.g. whether debaters' views caused audience members to strengthen or change their own opinions and how.

Dangers ▶

Dating Violence Prevention

The Facts

A video of your school's star player hitting a dating partner has been confiscated. Other schools in the district have players and partners involved in dating violence.

You are a member of an Athletic Personal Conduct Committee.
You are on one of the following sub-committees.

Definition Debaters: Define "What constitutes dating violence?"

One debater argues "Only physical contact which includes …"

_____

_____

One debater argues "All types of abuse which include …"

_____

_____

Policy Panelists - Formulate a *Personal Conduct Policy for Players.*

Describe expected behavior for players regarding dating partners:

_____

_____

Consequences for dating partner violence perpetrators:

_____

_____

Education and Prevention Planners - Develop a training program for players.

List topics in the program:

_____

_____

Counseling and referral suggestions for players involved in dating violence:

_____

_____

TEENS – ACTIONS, CONSEQUENCES, REWARDS

Dating Violence Prevention

FOR THE FACILITATOR

I. Purpose
To develop a simulated policy for sports players regarding dating violence; to heighten awareness about dating and sports-related violence: its problems, solutions, and prevention.

II. Skills
Define dating violence and other types of abuse.
Formulate at least two positive expectations and consequences for athletes and teens in general.
List at least two training topics and resources for teens at risk for, or involved in, dating violence.
Discuss and debate team member and opponent forms of abuse, the pros and cons of signing non-violence pledges, and banning from games abusive players and fans who are fighting.

III. Possible Activities
a. Encourage a brief discussion about people in sports or celebrities involved in domestic violence.
b. Explain that teens will practice being part of the solution – will have potential policy-making power.
c. Distribute the *Dating Violence Prevention* handout. Volunteers read the sections of the page aloud.
d. Allow teens to choose, or designate teens, for each of the three different sub-committees.
e. Debaters and sub-committee members sit close to each other to confer.
f. Each debater makes individual notes; each sub-committee designates a secretary to document their ideas.
g. The group re-convenes and debaters and subcommittee spokespeople share their conclusions.
h. Audience members provide additional suggestions and feedback.
   Possibilities
   - Definition Debaters "Only physical contact which includes …" hitting, punching, hair-pulling, spitting, unwanted touching or forced sexual contact; or "All types of abuse which include …" physical, emotional, verbal, spreading negative comments, gossip, or sexual content via social media texts and/or other privacy violations.
   - Policy Panelists "Expected behavior …" to treat dating partners with respect, e.g., no name-calling, put-downs, violence or abuse of any kind; "Consequences …" may range from suspension from games and/or school to being suspended from the team and/or expelled from school; counseling may be mandated.
   - Education and Prevention Planners "Topics" risk factors (violence at home, substance abuse, anger issues); warning signs (possessiveness, jealousy, stalking); "Counseling and referral suggestions" tell a trusted adult, seek counseling for anger and substance issues, research reliable websites (Dating Violence Prevention through The Department of Justice, Centers for Disease Control and Prevention, Find Youth Info, The White House, and other federally supported and state resources).
i. Ask teens to generalize "How would these definitions, policies, education, and prevention plans affect all teens, not just those on sports teams and their partners? (They would help promote safe, respectful relationships; let teens in troubled relationships know they are not alone; encourage abusers, and abused partners to seek help).

IV. Enrichment Activities
a. Ask teens to debate the pros and cons of athletes and/or all teens signing pledges to respect partners.
   Possibilities
   - Pros – may help teens who signed the pledge to uphold promises to themselves and others.
   - Cons – may be seen as just a piece of paper; does not address the root(s) of the problem.
b. Encourage a discussion about team member and opponent abuse, e.g., name-calling; racial, ethnic and sexual orientation slurs; violence on the field and locker room; fan fights in the parking lot.
c. Ask "Should players and fans involved in these abusive behaviors be banned from games? Why or why not?"

Dangers

Break the Bullying Cycle
The UN-interrupted Cycle

The person who bullies, the bystander, and the person who is bullied all have a role in perpetuating the cycle.

Place the letter of a statement that describes that person on the lines under 1), 2), 3).

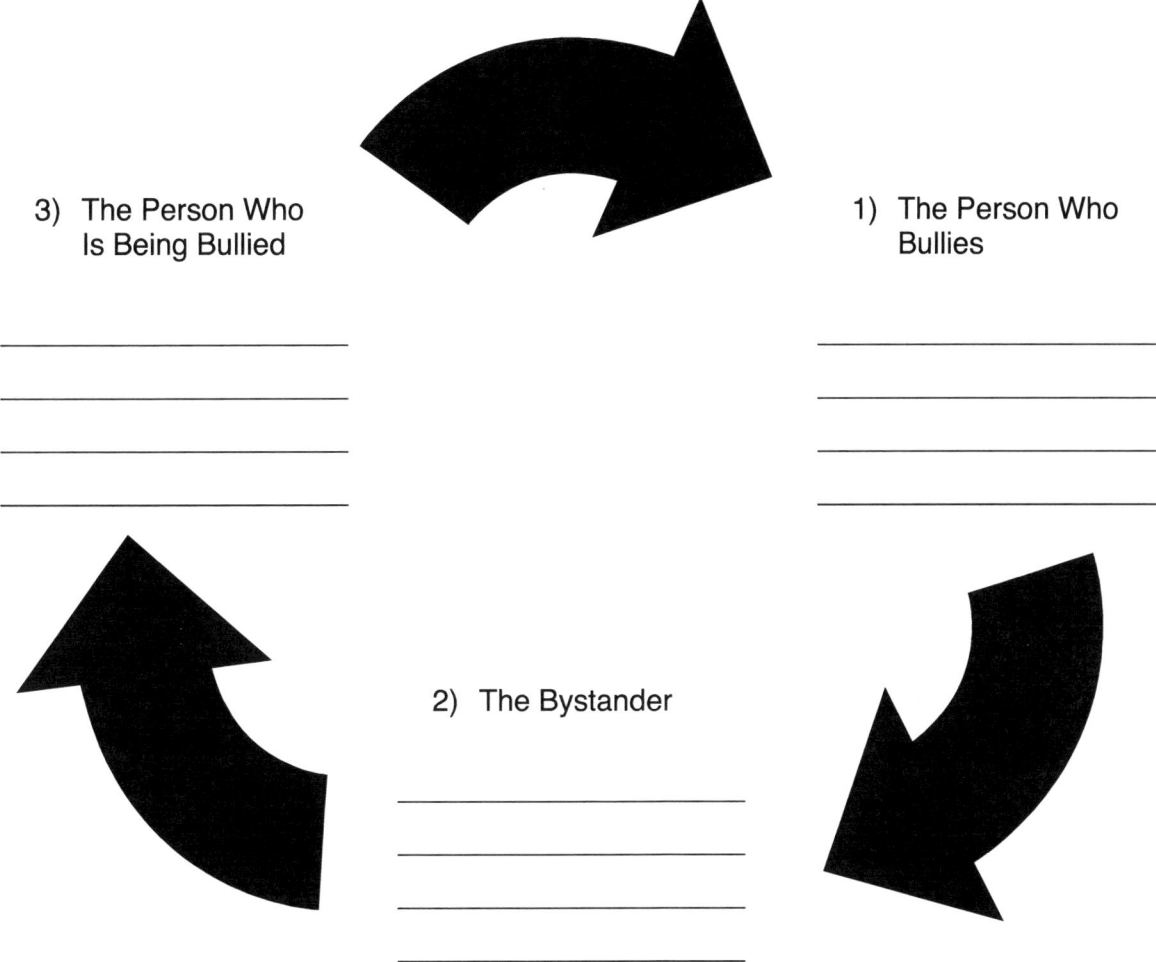

3) The Person Who Is Being Bullied

1) The Person Who Bullies

2) The Bystander

A. Grabs power.
B. "If I tell what I see it will worsen the situation."
C. "It's none of my business."
D. Seems different from me.
E. Is intolerant of anyone different than self.
F. Blames the potential victim.
G. Seems submissive.
H. "I'll be bullied next if I speak up."
I. Feels fearful and sad.
J. Likes to cause suffering.
K. "I'll be silent like everyone else."
L. May be envied or in competition with the person who bullies.

TEENS – ACTIONS, CONSEQUENCES, REWARDS

Break the Bullying Cycle

The IN-terrupted Cycle

The person who bullies, the bystander, and/or the person who is bullied can each break the cycle.

Place the letter that describes that person's empowering statement on each blank.

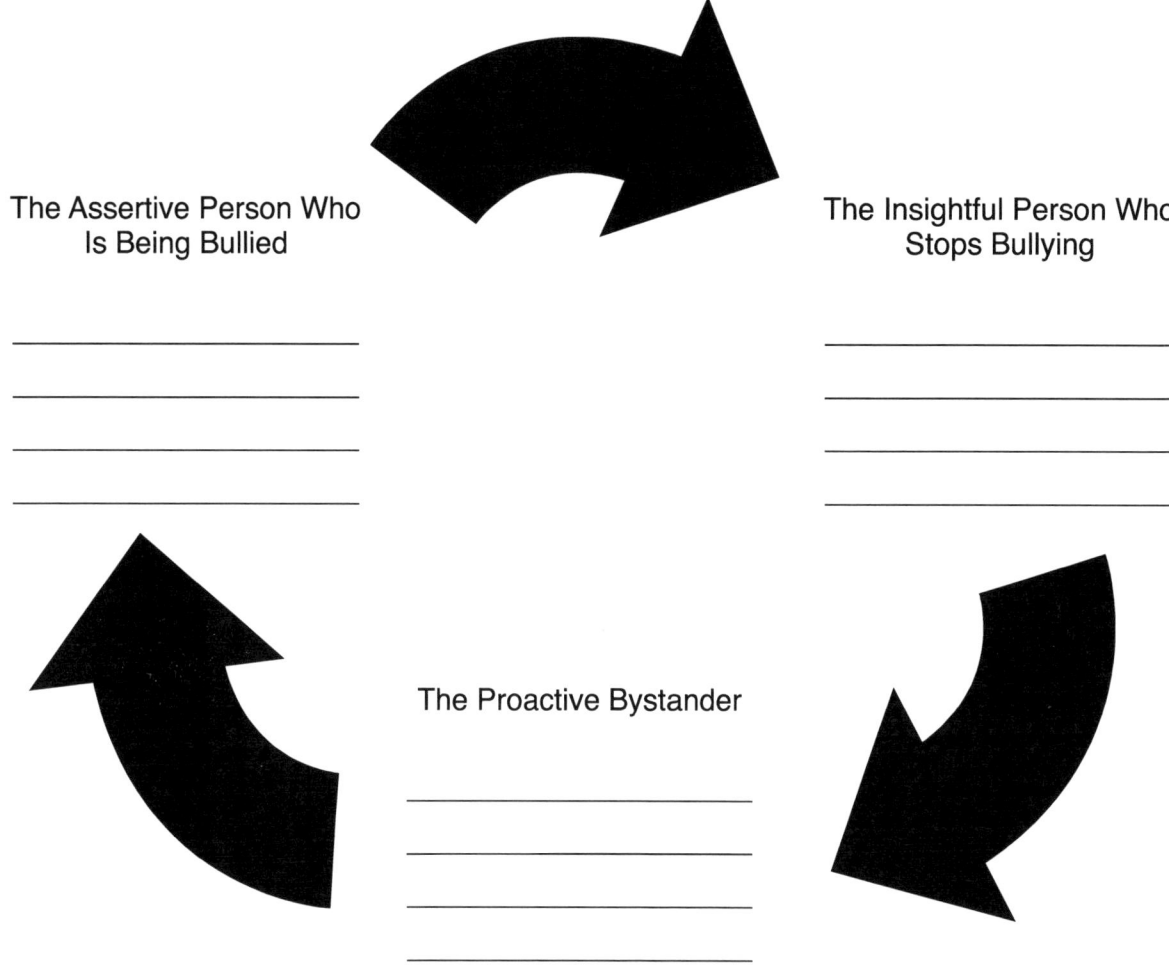

The Assertive Person Who Is Being Bullied

_____
_____
_____
_____

The Insightful Person Who Stops Bullying

_____
_____
_____
_____

The Proactive Bystander

_____
_____
_____

A. "I realize I'm taking my hurt out on an innocent person."
B. "I'll tell a trusted adult that I'm being disrespected."
C. "I can get help for anger management."
D. "While others do nothing, I'll tell a trusted adult."
E. "I'll defend the person being gossiped about."
F. "I'll take a self-defense class."
G. "I can recognize that we are all different in some way."
H. "I'll accept responsibility for my cruelty."
I. "It is my business."
J. "I will not turn my anger inward to self-harm."
K. "I'll say 'Stop!' and walk away."
L. "I'll never forward or respond to negative photos or messages."

Dangers

Break the Bullying Cycle

Consequences and Rewards

Imagine and list the consequences and rewards for each role.

Consequences for the Person Who Bullies	Consequences for the Bystander	Consequences for the Person Who Is Bullied
1. 2. 3.	1. 2. 3.	1. 2. 3.
Rewards for the Insightful Person Who Stops Bullying Others	**Rewards for the Proactive Bystander**	**Rewards for the Assertive Person Who Is Being Bullied**
1. 2. 3.	1. 2. 3.	1. 2. 3.

Respond confidentially to the sentence-starters.

My Private Insights

I am more often like (person who bullies, bystander, person who is bullied)

_____

I can do my part to break the bullying cycle by

_____
_____
_____
_____

TEENS – ACTIONS, CONSEQUENCES, REWARDS

Break the Bullying Cycle

FOR THE FACILITATOR

I. **Purpose**
To recognize that each person (the person who bullies, the person being bullied, and the bystander) has a role in perpetuating or interrupting the bullying cycle.

II. **Skills**
Identify four characteristics of, and three consequences for, each role that perpetuates the bullying cycle:
  The person who bullies others
  The bystander
  The person who is bullied
Identify four characteristics of and three rewards for each role that breaks the bullying cycle:
  The insightful person who stops bullying others
  The proactive bystander
  The assertive person who is bullied
Define own most frequent role and describe three ways to break the cycle.

III. **Possible Activities**
  a. Write "Cycle" on the board and ask its definition *(a recurring sequence of events)*.
  b. Explain that teens will focus on each person's role in the cycle of bullying.
  c. Distribute the *Break the Bullying Cycle* handouts – *The UN-interrupted Cycle, The IN-terrupted Cycle* and *Consequences and Rewards*. A volunteer reads the directions on each page aloud.
  d. Allow time for completion. Review responses.
  Answer Key
UN-interrupted Cycle Person who bullies A-E-F-J; Bystander B-C-H-K; Person who is bullied D-G-I-L
IN-terrupted Cycle Person who bullies A-C-G-H; Bystander D-E-I-L; Person who is bullied B-F-J-K
Consequences and Rewards Encourage teens to share responses. Elicit:
   • Consequences for person who bullies – less likely to keep friends; more likely to abuse other people and substances, and to commit crimes.
   • Consequences for bystander – contributes to the problem by providing an audience; guilt; acts powerless vs. helping to solve the problem.
   • Consequences for person who is bullied – sadness, fear, stress; nightmares; grades and work may suffer; low esteem; may turn to substances or harm self and/or others.
   • Rewards for insightful person who stops bullying – self-knowledge; courage to stop hurting people and one's own and others' reputations; sensitivity to one's own motives and others' feelings; less likely to become an abusive spouse or parent; relationships, grades and work may improve; may divert energy into productive purposes; may learn to cope with differences and manage anger.
   • Rewards for proactive bystander – empowerment; is part of the solution by discouraging the bullying behavior and/or defending person who is bullied; uses one's voice to speak out openly against bullying and/or behind the scenes to tell a trusted adult; helps promote a climate of physical and emotional safety vs. seeming to agree with bullying by remaining silent.
   • Rewards for assertive person who is bullied – practices standing up for oneself; awareness that self-worth comes from within and is not contingent on others' opinions; empowerment through telling trusted adults; empathy and ability to help others who are excluded or bullied.

IV. **Enrichment Activities**
  a. Write this *To Kill a Mockingbird* quote by Harper Lee on the board:
  "You never really understand a person until you consider things from his point of view … until you climb into his skin and walk around in it."
  b. Ask how this wisdom would benefit each of the following: the person who bullies, the bystander and the person who is bullied.

ATTRIBUTES 5

*Two qualities are indispensible:
first, an intellect that, even in the darkest hour,
retains some glimmering of the inner light which leads to truth;
and second, the courage to follow this faint light wherever it may lead.*
~ Carl von Clausewitz

Health-A-Gories .... page 83-84 ▶
Teens specify healthy rewards and unhealthy consequences regarding nutrition, exercise and sleep, and in emotional, recreational, spiritual, vocational, intellectual, social, financial, and other aspects of life.

Transparency Game .... page 87 ▶
Teens participate in a game to differentiate between transparency and hidden agendas and describe their consequences and rewards. Teens present skits and peers identify ulterior motives.

Rebelling? Now, Try Renovating! .... page 89 ▶
Teens direct analytical and independent thinking skills into productive and innovative purposes. Teens discuss consequences of both rebellion and blind acceptance and practice steps toward peaceful change.

REMINDER:
Save completed handouts in "My Actions Book" (see pages 11-14)

Chapter 5 - Attributes Behavioral Coping Skills

Throughout the chapter, teens will communicate through oral, written and creative expression and give and receive feedback.

Teens: Skills in each activity.
Facilitators: Competencies to evaluate.

Health-A-Gories
- State rewards and consequences in twelve health-related categories.
- State one or more actions in each category to promote rewards and avoid consequences.

Transparency Game
- Write sixteen examples of transparency and of hidden agendas in game board boxes.
- Discriminate between transparency and ulterior motive examples by shading the hidden agendas.
- State three or more situations in which transparency is not appropriate.

Rebelling? Now, Try Renovating!
- Discuss reasons a rule seems ridiculous or is reality-based.
- State a rule to try to change.
- Take six steps to revise the rule.
- Practice two or more steps to spread the word and gather support.

Health-A-Gories
Part I

Each team fills in the horizontal row of boxes for their specific category.

Health-A-Gory	Do	Rewards	Do Not	Consequences
Nutrition Team				
Exercise Team				
Sleep Team				
Hygiene Team				
Mental Health Team				
Recreation Team				

TEENS – ACTIONS, CONSEQUENCES, REWARDS

Health-A-Gories
Part II

Each team fills in the horizontal row of boxes for their specific category.

Health-A-Gory	Do	Rewards	Do Not	Consequences
Spirituality Team				
Vocational Team				
Intellectual Team				
Social Team				
Financial Team				
"Other" Team				

Attributes ▶

Health-A-Gories

FOR THE FACILITATOR

I. Purpose
To identify healthy actions and their rewards, and unhealthy actions and their consequences.

II. Skills
State two or more positive behaviors, their rewards, and actions to avoid and their consequences regarding the following aspects of health:
- Exercise
- Financial
- Hygiene
- Intellectual
- Mental Health
- Nutrition
- Recreation
- Sleep
- Social
- Spirituality
- Vocational
- Other (can be sexual health, volunteerism, creativity, or a different topic at the facilitator's discretion).

III. Possible Activities
a. Write "Health-A-Gories" on the board and ask what it means (health-related categories).
b. Explain that teens will play a game.
   Team Format
   - Distribute the *Health-A-Gories Part I and Part II* handouts.
   - Divide teens into teams; designate topics or allow teens to choose topics.
   - Teams will fill in the horizontal row of boxes across the page for their topic(s).
   - If the group is small, individuals or small teams will each take more than one topic.
   - Team members confer and a secretary writes their ideas on a handout.
   - The group re-convenes, secretaries share their teams' responses, and receive feedback.
   Board Activity Format
   - Copy both of the *Health-A-Gories* handouts, pages 83 and 84 onto the board.
   - Ask the group to brainstorm responses as volunteers fill in the horizontal rows on the board.
c. Suggested responses for *Health-A-Gories for the Facilitator* are started below and continue page 88.

IV. Enrichment Activities
a. Encourage teens to think about additional categories for the "Other" Team row.
b. A team may complete the row of boxes on the handout or the Board Activity format may be used.

Health-A-Gory	Do	Rewards	Do Not	Consequences
Nutirition Team	Eat a variety of food: vegetables, proteins, and grains.	Healthy weight; healthy body.	Eat too many processed, sweet, and fatty foods.	Over or under-weight; poor health.
Exercise Team	Find activities one enjoys and do them daily.	Muscle tone; more energy; weight in line with body build.	Become inactive; spend too much time watching TV, games, etc.	Poor muscle tone; low energy; weight problems.

(Continued on the next page)

TEENS – ACTIONS, CONSEQUENCES, REWARDS

Health-A-Gories (continued)
FOR THE FACILITATOR

Health-A-Gory	Do	Rewards	Do Not	Consequences
Sleep Team	Have eight or more hours of sleep; turn off phone, TV, etc. at bedtime.	Alert at school, work and at the wheel; more stable emotionally.	Nap late in the day; engage in heated debates at bedtime.	Tired; poor performance in school; irritability.
Hygiene Team	Shower daily; use deodorant; fresh clothes; brush and floss teeth at least twice daily.	Look and smell good; present a cared-for and self-respecting image that helps with peers, employers, teachers, etc.	Neglect hair, body, nails or teeth; wear unclean, torn, or wrinkled clothes.	Look and smell bad; give the impression of not caring about oneself.
Mental Health Team	Share feelings with trusted people; ask for help for moods and issues; avoid alcohol and drugs; think *possibility thoughts*.	Cope with challenges; function at one's best; discover how *possibility thinking* leads to positive feelings and actions.	Keep secrets and suffer in silence; think that asking for help is a weakness; focus on what one *can't* do.	Depressed, angry and/or anxious feelings; may harm self or others; not function at one's optimal level.
Recreation Team	Balance school, work and family responsibilities with relaxation and leisure activities.	Renewal; creativity; better able to focus at school and work after a break.	Think recreation is a waste of time or that rejuvenation is unnecessary.	Burnout from pushing oneself too hard and not renewing energy through recreation.
Spirituality Team	Reach out and rely on one's spirit; tap into inner strength; be inspired by nature, the arts, etc.	Belief in one's own spirit; true to self; positive thoughts about oneself and the future.	Become negative, hopeless and helpless; believe the worst; expect failure; distrust oneself and others.	Sadness; negative views of oneself and the world; feelings of inadequacy to face challenges alone.
Vocational Team	Find one's passion and pursue it; plan related educational and volunteer or work opportunities.	Career that meets one's individual needs (creativity, helping others, productivity) and financial needs.	Choose an occupation solely for its financial rewards or because someone else advises it.	Hours of discomfort every week and looking forward only to days off and paychecks; no job satisfaction.
Intellectual Team	Attend school regularly; pay attention in class; complete assignments promptly; ask for help from teacher or tutor.	Develop one's academic and "hands-on" interests and skills and excel in those; obtain help to pass difficult subjects.	Talk, text or be distracted in class; ignore assignments; make half-hearted efforts; fail to ask for help; skip classes.	Poor grades, fewer options for post-high school training or college; not finding one's future passion or what one does best.
Social Team	Find like-minded and supportive friends and partner(s); achieve a balance among independence, dependence and interdependence.	Enjoy true friendships and healthy dating relationships that foster empathy and consideration for others; develop assertiveness.	Associate with negative people who put one down or drag one down with pessimism, alcohol and drugs or other unhealthy behaviors.	Become like the negative people, too clingy or unwilling to think for oneself; develop low esteem and unhealthy physical and mental habits.
Financial Team	Make a budget and stick to it; find ways to increase earnings and save money but do not let a race for wealth dominate one's life.	Respect money without worshipping wealth; self-discipline, (save for a goal or know that better grades now will lead to more career options later.)	Spend more than one earns; borrow recklessly; sacrifice school for cash; try to impress others or measure one's worth in money.	Lack of self-discipline regarding money; debt; thinking money "buys" friends or that one's identity is defined by what one owns, drives, wears, etc.

Attributes ▶

Transparency Game

Transparent:
see-through, crystal clear; authentic. (What you see is what you get.)
Hidden agenda:
ulterior motive; fake. (I pretend to be your friend; but I have my reasons.)

Practice Instructions
Shade in the hidden agenda examples.

Do this favor. I'll be your friend.	I really like this person.	This partner will impress people.
I admit I made a mistake.	Flatter teacher. Hope for an *A*.	I respect people's differences.
Pretend I have money.	Help grandpa and he'll pay me.	Befriend someone with a car.

Game Board Instructions
Create a game board.
Write an example of transparency or a hidden agenda in each box.

Hints

Transparency
Make wishes perfectly clear.
Admit limitations; acknowledge strengths.
Be truthful but tactful.
Act with honest motives.

Hidden agenda
Hide or hint about one's wishes.
Boast falsely about oneself.
Flatter to earn points.
Manipulate to get one's own way.

Game Board

Creator's code name _____

Later you will pass the paper to your players.
Later your players will shade in the hidden agendas and leave the transparent examples crystal clear.

TEENS – ACTIONS, CONSEQUENCES, REWARDS

Transparency Game

FOR THE FACILITATOR

I. Purpose
To promote transparency, discourage hidden agendas; discuss rewards, consequences, and exceptions.

II. Skills
Differentiate among nine examples – six hidden agendas and three examples of transparency.
Create sixteen examples – some of hidden agendas and some of transparency.
Identify peers' examples of transparency and hidden agendas.
State at least three rewards of transparency and three consequences of hidden agendas.
Discuss at least three situations in which transparency is not recommended.

III. Possible Activities
a. Point to a window and ask about its main characteristic (see through, transparent).
b. Ask what it means for a person to be transparent (honest, genuine).
c. Explain that teens will create and play a game about transparency and ulterior motives.
d. Distribute the *Transparency Game* handout; a volunteer reads the definitions and Practice Instructions aloud.
e. Teens shade in the hidden agenda boxes and then put pencils down (do not proceed further).
   Correct shadings
   Column 1 – top and bottom, column 2 – middle and bottom, column 3 – top and bottom.
f. Volunteers read the Game Board Instructions and Hints aloud. Teens document their code names.
g. Set a time limit to allow teens to complete as many boxes as possible and still have time for the game.
h. Teens put pencils down when all boxes are filled; teens **do not** shade their own boxes!
i. Teens may not have time to fill in all boxes; the game can still proceed as described below.
   - Teens pass their papers to the person on their right if sitting in a circle; behind them if in rows.
   - Players quickly shade in **one** hidden agenda and pass the paper to the next person.
   - When all boards are complete game board creators claim their papers.
   - Creators share whether the shaded boxes reflect their hidden agenda examples; if not, why not.
   - Encourage respectful debate and open-minded discussion about disputed boxes.
   - Remind teens no one loses the game; all players think, collaborate, learn and win.
j. Ask teens to brainstorm situations in which transparency is not appropriate.
   Possibilities
   - Do not reveal personal data that could lead a dangerous person to oneself or others.
   - Do not disclose family or financial info unless appropriate, e.g., a college Financial Aid office.
   - Do not display explicit photos or private information that can be forwarded or misused.
k. Ask about rewards of appropriate transparency (true to oneself, gain trust, perceived as loyal).
l. Ask about consequences of hidden agendas (not true to oneself, perceived as a sneaky, others eventually see through the façade).

IV. Enrichment Activities
a. Teens form small groups to plan brief skits exemplifying transparency and hidden agendas.
b. Cast members perform and audience members guess if transparency or hidden agendas were enacted.
c. Audience members identify the suspected ulterior motives for hidden agendas.

Attributes

Rebelling? *Now, Try Renovating!*

People often disagree about rules. Here is an example of a possible controversial rule: "Students may not tell others when they are accepted into college."

1. What's your opinion about this rule?
   _____

2. What do you think was the reality-based reason for the rule?
   _____

3. What happens when you violate a rule that you do not agree with …
   at home? _____ at school? _____ in society? _____

4. What would happen if everyone blindly followed every rule?
   _____

5. What would happen if everyone rebelled against every rule?
   _____

6. What would happen if people with a good reason to rebel, did nothing about it?
   _____

7. What can be done about rules you disagree with?
   _____

8. Why do you think teens are more likely than younger children to question rules?
   _____

If you're rebelling, renovate! What is a rule you would like the rule-makers to reconsider?
_____

Follow these steps below:

Research the rule's exact wording and intent.
_____

Research the rule's basis – possibly became a rule because of a one-time occurrence, it was needed at the time, or created because of something valid you're not aware of.
_____

Specify why you disagree with the rule.
_____

If you want to abolish the rule, state your reasons.
_____

If you want to change the rule, state your suggested revisions.
_____

Note details about prior or current efforts to renovate the rule.
_____

TEENS – ACTIONS, CONSEQUENCES, REWARDS

Rebelling? *Now, Try Renovating!*

FOR THE FACILITATOR

I. Purpose
To validate teens' needs to test authority, to develop an independent identity, analytical and decision-making skills; to respectfully disagree and direct these needs into productive and innovative purposes.

II. Skills
State reasons for disagreement with a theoretical rule.
Note the rule's possible reality-based reason.
Identify three consequences of violating rules.
Predict the worst outcomes of blind acceptance or of total rebellion against all rules.
Describe what can be done about rules disagreed with.
Identify three reasons teens tend to question or rebel against authority.
Define a rule that rule-makers need to reconsider.
Complete six preliminary steps to attempt to peacefully change that specific rule.

III. Possible Activities
a. Before the session, obtain a school handbook if teens want to look up the wording of a rule.
b. Encourage teens to recall rules they disagree with; list a few on the board.
c. Ask about the rules' reasons (safety, based on a need, appropriate at the time, over-reaction).
d. Distribute the *Rebelling? Now, Try Renovating!* handout to teams or individuals:
   A volunteer reads the rule at the top aloud; teens write or respond orally to the numbered questions and stop at the bold text.
   Possibilities
   1. Disagree because most teens are bursting to share the good news.
   2. Reality-based to spare the feelings of teens who did not yet receive acceptance letters.
   3. Violate a rule at home – grounded; at school – suspended; in society – arrested, etc.
   4. If everyone blindly followed rules, no reformation would occur.
   5. If everyone rebelled, anarchy would result.
   6. Rules can often be changed.
   7. Teens question rules to test authority, to develop an identity, analytical and decision making skills. Young children often listen to adults without question.
e. Allow time for individuals, teams, or the group as a whole to identify a rule they would like rule-makers to reconsider and complete the six steps.
f. Expect a variety of responses based on teens' interests in school rules, community or society laws.

IV. Enrichment Activities
a. With the administration's permission, encourage teens to move forward and mount posters, distribute flyers, make announcements, etc.
b. With parental/caregiver permission, teens who selected community or society issues may proceed, with legal access, to public places to legally post, distribute and present information.

CIRCUMSTANCES 6

*There is no easy way out of our circumstances...
Sometimes you stick it out even when you want to give up because you know that on the other side is either a better situation or a better you.*

~ Krissi Dallas

FUNction Junction .... page 93-95 ▶

Teens identify rules and family roles that may indicate dysfunctional dynamics. Teens replace unhealthy admonitions with self-affirmations, depict and/or describe their FUNctional behavior.

EVERYONE IS DIFFERENT FROM ME, BUT CAN BE SIMILAR! .... page 97 ▶

Teens note how people who look different may be similar in important ways. Teens discuss the consequences of discrimination and explore ways differences and similarities enrich one's experiences.

OSTRICH OR EINSTEIN? .... page 99 ▶

Teens acknowledge and explore ways to solve a current problem and to prevent a potential problem. Teens discuss the dangers of hiding or ignoring problems and ways to avoid temptations.

NOBLE NOBEL .... page 101 ▶

Teens personalize the 17-year old Nobel Peace Prize Laureate's words "One child, one teacher, one book, one pen can change the world … when the whole world is silent, even one voice becomes powerful."

Academics .... page 103-105 ▶

Teens practice ways to reduce academic stress, reinforce time spent on homework and use active study techniques. Teens explore ways to promote adequate sleep and note its effects on school performance.

You Can Help No Matter What! .... page 107 ▶

Teens describe ways to help in appropriate settings and decide when it's best to not help. Teens create scenarios, list options and point out the positive and negative results of each.

REMINDER:
Save completed handouts in "My Actions Book" (see pages 11-14)

Chapter 6 - Circumstances Behavioral Coping Skills

Throughout the chapter, teens will communicate through oral, written and creative expression and give and receive feedback.

Teens: Skills in each activity.
Facilitators: Competencies to evaluate.

FUNction Junction
- Enact, identify or observe twenty-five pantomimes of dysfunctional and functional rules and roles.
- Substitute sixteen self-affirming statements for sixteen dysfunctional rules.
- Draw and share what will be thought, felt and done after replacing dysfunction with FUNction.

Everyone is Different from Me, but Can be Similar!
- Draw a person who is different from self.
- Label the brain with own thoughts.
- Label the heart with own feelings.
- Identify three differences that are small compared to similarities.
- Discuss three or more ways people suffer from discrimination and benefit from acceptance.
- Note that people who are different on the outside may be similar inside and vice versa.

Ostrich or Einstein?
- State a problem that has been concealed.
- Depict and/or describe three or more ways to solve the problem and/or seek help.
- Depict and/or describe at least three ways to prevent the problem, if it was preventable.

Noble Nobel
- State at least two facts about the Nobel Peace Prize and its 17-year old 2014 winner.
- Identify a difficult circumstance being faced or that others endure.
- Depict and/or describe five or more ways to advocate for people in similar situations.
- Take the first step to promote a cause.

Academics
- Plot own level of stress on a 10-point scale in seven scholastic achievement categories.
- Identify six or more positive reinforcers and use them as homework rewards.
- Gradually increase time on task and attention span.
- Practice a self-quiz technique to improve focus and retention.
- Demonstrate mnemonics to memorize facts.
- State at least two academic consequences of sleep deprivation and two rewards of adequate sleep.

You Can Help No Matter What!
- Discriminate between two positive and two negative ways to handle exclusion.
- Identify three positive ways to help and one evading action in a scenario about feeling inadequate.
- Describe a predicament with four options for peers to contemplate.
- Point out positive and negative results from among four options for each peer-created scenario.
- Name five or more situations in which it is not advisable to help.

Circumstances

FUNction Junction
Rules and Roles Charades

RULE	RULE	ROLE	RULE	RULE
Zip your lip to show "Don't talk."	Shake your head "No" to show "Deny what's going on."	Pat someone's head, pretend to help someone stand up to show a person excessively caring for others.	Point to your head then make speaking motions with your mouth to show "Talk about your thoughts."	Cup your hand around your ear as if listening. Move your mouth as if talking to show "Communicate."
RULE Point to your heart. Push your hands down to stuff your feelings to show "Don't express emotions."	**ROLE** Hang your head. Point to yourself to show a person who accepts blame for all family problems.	**ROLE** Make an angry facial expression and kick the air to show a person who acts out in anger.	**RULE** Point to your heart, then make talking motions with your mouth to show "Talk about your feelings."	**RULE** Ask a peer to help: Close your eyes as the person leads you around to show "Trust people who are trustworthy."
RULE Pretend to lock doors and close curtains to show "Keep outsiders out."	**ROLE** "A – A – A – A" Write on the board to show that "My job is to make everyone proud."	**ROLE** Nod your head "Yes" and show a fake smile to show the person who tries to keep everyone happy.	**RULE** Pretend to open a door and shake someone's hand to show "Welcome helpful outsiders."	**RULE** Stand in the center then draw a square around your spot to show "Maintain appropriate boundaries."
RULE Place hands at sides of your mouth and pretend to whisper to show "Keep secrets."	**RULE** Crouch into a corner with your arms crossed to show a person who hides.	**RULE** Make a question mark in the air, then shake your head "No" to show "Don't ask questions."	**RULE** Point at someone then hit your pointing finger and shake your head "No" to show "Don't blame people."	**RULE** Point to your head and heart then open your arms and mouth words to show "Share your thoughts and feelings."
RULE Point a finger to show "Blame others."	**ROLE** Laugh excessively and act silly to show a person who provides humor or a clown.	**RULE** Point to your head, nod "Yes," mouth the word "Aha!" and make a light bulb motion to show "Gain insight."	**RULE** Crouch in a corner then get up, stand tall, take a deep breath and walk forward to show "Face problems."	**RULE** Pretend to look in a mirror then pat yourself on the back to show "Value yourself."

© 2015 WHOLE PERSON ASSOCIATES, 101 W. 2ND ST., SUITE 203, DULUTH MN 55802 • 800-247-6789

TEENS – ACTIONS, CONSEQUENCES, REWARDS

FUNction Junction
Self-Affirmations

Affirm: to declare positively that something is true.

Write the letter matching each Affirmation in front of each Harmful Rule.

HARMFUL RULES	AFFIRMATIONS TO TELL MYSELF
Ex: You'll never amount to anything.	Ex: I'll make the most of myself.
1. You must make the family look good.	A. I weigh pros and cons and consider advice from trusted people.
2. Don't rock the boat.	B. I value my perceptions but am open to others' views.
3. Do as I say, not as I do.	C. My past does not predict my future.
4. Express only positive feelings.	D. I find unconditional support in myself, trusted people and a higher power.
5. You should never get angry.	E. I work for win-win conflict resolution or agree to disagree.
6. Do what's expected, no matter what.	F. I ask a trusted adult for help.
7. Never question my behavior.	G. I make positive changes despite obstacles.
8. Your needs are not as important as mine.	H. I take care of myself and help others when appropriate.
9. You must take care of everyone.	I. My needs are important but I do consider others' needs.
10. I'll sabotage your efforts to change.	J. I question behavior that I don't understand.
11. Don't ask an outsider for help.	K. I do what's expected if it reflects my beliefs.
12. Avoid or fear conflict.	L. I learn productive ways to cope with anger.
13. I'm not here for you if you disappoint me.	M. I express feelings honestly but considerately.
14. You are ruined for life.	N. My actions reflect my values.
15. You're clueless about what's happening.	O. I rock the boat respectfully when changes are needed.
16. You can't make a decision without me.	P. I do my best for me and my family.

Circumstances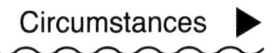

FUNction Junction
Have F U N ction!

Depict and/or describe what you think your life would be like with FUNction.

FUNction Junction

FOR THE FACILITATOR

I. Purpose
To overcome dysfunctional rules, roles and lifestyles, and function optimally.

II. Skills
Enact, identify or observe up to twenty-five pantomimes of dysfunctional and functional rules and roles.
Replace sixteen unhealthy rules with healthy self-affirmations.
Depict and describe what will be thought, felt and done when dysfunction is replaced with FUNction.

III. Possible Activities
a. Ask teens the meaning of *junction* (crossroads).
b. Encourage a discussion of unhealthy dynamics (related to addiction, abuse, etc.).
c. Question teens "What would be a crossroad?" (where harmful situations and self-affirming thoughts and actions meet).
d. Ask about the effects of an unhealthy situation (problems with grades, emotions and relationships).
e. Pose the question "What can a person in an unhealthy situation do?"
Elicit that teens can choose to be victims or over-comers; they can suffer in silence or ask for help.

Rules and Roles Charades
- Make one photocopy and cut out the boxes.
- Place cutouts face down in a stack.
- Teens take turns picking up a cutout, reading the bold heading aloud and portraying the rule/role with body language; peers guess the rule/role.

Self-Affirmations
- A volunteer reads the directions aloud.
- Distribute the handout and allow time for completion
- Encourage teens to share responses.

Responses Answer Key

1. P	5. L	9. H	13. D
2. O	6. K	10. G	14. C
3. N	7. J	11. F	15. B
4. M	8. I	12. E	16. A

Have FUNction – expect individual responses; teens share their papers and receive peer feedback.

IV. Enrichment Activities
Encourage teens to write poems or lyrics about FUNctioning.

Circumstances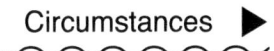

EVERYONE IS DIFFERENT FROM ME, BUT CAN BE SIMILAR!

1. On the left, draw the outline of a fictitious person, allowing plenty of room in the head and body.

2. Draw hair very different from yours.

3. Add facial features very different from yours.

4. Draw a large empty brain in the head.

5. Draw a large empty heart in the chest.

6. Fill the brain with thoughts that matter most to YOU.

7. Fill the heart with YOUR strongest emotions.

What do you know about the person that you have drawn?

_____

_____

_____

TEENS – ACTIONS, CONSEQUENCES, REWARDS

Everyone is Different from Me, but Can be Similar!

FOR THE FACILITATOR

I. Purpose
To note that people who look different from us may be similar in important ways.
To discuss consequences of discrimination against people who seem "different."
To describe ways that differences and similarities among people enrich the human experience.

II. Skills
Draw a person whose body build, hair and facial features are very different from oneself.
Attribute own thoughts and feelings to the person being drawn.
Acknowledge that someone who looks very different may be very much like self and vice versa.
Identify three visible and invisible differences that are minor compared to similarities among people.
Discuss three ways students and societies suffer from discrimination and benefit from acceptance.

III. Possible Activities
a. Ask teens to recall kids' magazine pages where they found differences and similarities in two pictures.
b. Explain that they will focus on differences and similarities among people.
c. Distribute the *Everyone is Different from Me, but Can be Similar!* handout; a volunteer reads the instructions aloud.
d. Remind teens that artistic ability or perfect spelling or grammar is not needed for this activity.
e. Ask teens to consider sensitivity of others in the room and not to depict anyone who would have hurt feelings.
f. Allow time for completion.
g. Preview drawings to ensure teens do not share a drawing about which a peer may be sensitive.
h. Encourage teens to share their drawings (if they would not offend anyone in the group).
i. Ask teens to share what they know about the persons they drew.
Elicit that their person may look different on the outside but is very similar inside.
j. Suggest that teens brainstorm differences that are readily noticed.
Possibilities
Height, weight, racial or ethnic features, physical conditions e.g., in a wheelchair or elderly.
k. Suggest that teens brainstorm differences that may not be visible.
Possibilities
Learning difficulties; physical issues; unwanted thoughts, feelings or behaviors; substance abuse.
l. Write "People are more alike than different" on the board.
m. Ask "How would belief in this statement impact schools and society?"
Elicit that people who experience depression, anxiety, fear, loneliness, etc. from mistreatment would feel accepted; bullying, bigotry, exclusion, narrow-minded cliques, etc. would diminish.

IV. Enrichment Activities
a. On the back of the handout instruct teens to draw someone with an outward appearance similar to theirs.
 - Tell them to insert into the brain thoughts very different from theirs.
 - Tell them to insert into the heart feelings very different from theirs.
 - Ask about their conclusions
Elicit that people who look like them may be very different inside.
b. Ask about the value of associating with people who have similar thoughts and feelings.
Elicit that they have common interests and beliefs and may enjoy the same activities.
c. Ask about the benefits of associating with people who have very different thoughts and feelings.
Elicit that teens expand their awareness of other viewpoints, cultures, etc.

Circumstances

OSTRICH OR EINSTEIN?

An ostrich hides from a problem.

In the sand, draw and/or describe a problem you need to stop hiding or hiding *from*.

A clever person solves a problem... ~ Albert Einstein

Share ways you can solve the above problem and/or seek help.

... A wise person avoids it. ~ Albert Einstein

Could that problem have been avoided or prevented? Explain.

OSTRICH OR EINSTEIN?

FOR THE FACILITATOR

I. Purpose
To acknowledge and plan ways to solve a current problem; to avoid a potential problem.

II. Skills
Differentiate among hiding, hiding from, and preventing problems.
Label a current problem that has been concealed.
Depict and/or describe three or more ways to solve it and/or to seek help.
Depict and/or describe at least three ways to prevent the problem, if it was preventable.

III. Possible Activities
a. Write "hide" on the board and ask its meaning (put out of sight or conceal).
b. Write "avoid" on the board and ask its meaning (prevent; keep away from someone or something).
c. Ask about ostrich myths and sayings (that they stick their heads in the sand and ignore problems).
d. Explain that ostriches do not bury their heads – when in danger they lay their heads and necks on the ground and are camouflaged by the same color sand; bodies look like bushes and may fool predators.
e. Distribute the *Ostrich or Einstein?* handout and explain that teens will pretend to be the ostrich.
f. A volunteer reads the captions, quotations and directions aloud.
g. Before teens start drawing and/or writing, explain that teens may be …
   - Hiding a situation, e.g., that they are being abused
   - Hiding an internal trait, e.g., jealousy
   - Hiding *from* a circumstance or person, e.g., an unhealthy relationship or a bully
h. Allow time for completion.
i. Encourage teens to share their responses and receive peer feedback.
j. Expect a variety of individual responses.
   Possibilities for teens who need prompts to personalize:
   - Ways to solve problems – admit the problem, brainstorm options and weigh pros and cons of each, select the best option, and stick to a plan; if it proves unsatisfactory, try a different option.
   - Sources of help – trusted adults, medical and mental health professionals, support groups and resources that are considered safe and reliable by trusted adults and professionals.

IV. Enrichment Activities
Encourage teens to research Albert Einstein's biography and quotations, and apply them to their lives.

Circumstances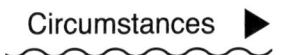

NOBLE NOBEL – One Can Change the World

Malala Yousafzai, 17, was the youngest Nobel Peace Prize Laureate as of 2014.
She wrote *I Am Malala: The Girl Who Stood Up for Education and Was Shot by the Taliban.**
Speeches at the United Nations and Harvard show that she speaks louder after efforts to silence her.

**"One child, one teacher, one book, one pen, can change the world …
When the whole world is silent, even one voice becomes powerful."**

You, like Malala, can be a victor, not a victim.
Do you have unfortunate circumstances to overcome and/or a heart to help?

I am one person. I have one pen. I have one voice. What will I do?

* Malala, from Pakistan, shared the Nobel Peace Prize
with Kailash Satyarthi, human rights activist from India.
She wrote the book in collaboration with British journalist Christina Lamb.

TEENS – ACTIONS, CONSEQUENCES, REWARDS

NOBLE NOBEL – One Can Change the World

FOR THE FACILITATOR

I. Purpose
To gain inspiration from a teen role model who turned tragedy into triumph.
To identify how to turn a personal setback into a triumph.

II. Skills
State at least two basic facts about the Nobel Peace Prize and its 17-year old 2014 winner.
Identify a difficult situation being faced or an unfortunate circumstance that others endure.
Depict and/or describe at least five ways to advocate for people who suffer under similar conditions.
Take the first step to promote a cause.

III. Possible Activities
a. Write "Noble Nobel" on the board and discuss their meanings.
   - NOBLE – righteous.
   - NOBEL – Alfred Nobel, born in Sweden; chemist, engineer and innovator who was concerned about how he would be remembered because dynamite was one of his inventions.
   - Dynamite is helpful in construction, mining, etc. and not always used to harm people.
   - He willed his wealth to fund Nobel Prizes.
   - The categories of the Nobel Peace Prize are Physics, Chemistry, Medicine, Literature, Peace, and Economic Sciences.

b. Distribute the *Noble Nobel - One Can Change the World* handout; a volunteer reads the text aloud.

c. Encourage teens to depict or describe five aspects and/or actions regarding their advocacy cause.
   - Suggest cartoons, collages, symbols, sketches, poems, essays, news articles, journal entries, etc.
   - Emphasize that their papers are private unless they wish to share.
   - Teens may use their own past or present traumatic situations as an impetus to help others.
   - Teens not in crises may be motivated by what they have witnessed, heard or read about.

d. Allow time for completion.

e. Encourage teens to share their responses and receive peer feedback.

   Possible ways to advocate for a cause
   - Read reports and watch news about the issue
   - Research what is and is not being done for the cause
   - Call and/or write to governmental agencies and leaders
   - Blog, write editorials, make videos about the issue
   - Work or volunteer for the cause
   - Recruit like-minded people to join one's efforts

IV. Enrichment Activities
a. Teams or individuals research a topic related to Nobel Prizes, their recipients, or teen advocates, and report to the group.

   Possible Topics
   - CNN Films' *Girl Rising* about girls across the globe and how education can change the world
   - Biography of Alfred Nobel
   - Biography of Malala Yousafzai, Kailash Satyarthi and other Nobel Laureates
   - Nobel Prizes in various categories
   - Teens who advocate for humanitarianism, start charities or write about causes for concern

b. Encourage teens to discuss their possible causes and the first steps they'll take to promote their causes.

c. Suggest that teens identify personal setbacks.

d. Ask them to share the ways they have in the past, or could in the future, turn this into a triumph.

Circumstances

Academics
Stress Graph

Place an "x" to mark your stress level in each column.
Draw lines to connect the "x's" to plot your stress graph.
Describe a way to handle each issue at the bottom of the columns.

Ratings 1 = none 10 = most	Ex: "x" aligned with 8 = much stress	Feel pressure about grades	Feel pressure at home and/or work	Feel fear of being disliked due to grades	Feel snowed under. Don't know where to start	Think there is never enough time	Experience difficulty being organized	Experience problems focusing on the work
1								
2								
3								
4								
5								
6								
7								
8	x							
9								
10								
How to handle each issue ➡								

© 2015 WHOLE PERSON ASSOCIATES, 101 W. 2ND ST., SUITE 203, DULUTH MN 55802 • 800-247-6789

TEENS – ACTIONS, CONSEQUENCES, REWARDS

Academics – Timely Rewards

Piece workers are paid for each piece of work or action performed.
Use the same method to reward yourself for homework time.
Use the table below to track your progress.

Date	HOMEWORK Document work accomplished. *Example: Wrote essay*	TIME SPENT Increase work intervals every two days. *Example: Ten, then twenty minute intervals*	REWARD Document your break time. *Example: Texted*

How did this work out for you?

_____

_____

_____

Circumstances

Academics – Techniques

Quiz Yourself

Have you ever read a page out of a textbook and then forgotten the content?
You wasted your time and received no benefit.
Try this way to stay focused and retain information.

1. Choose a page you may be tested on soon.
2. Read the text and create a "Fill in the Blanks" self-test.

Example of text:

> "Prom-posal"
> Teens have more pressure than ever related to proms. A "prom-posal" is an elaborate way of asking someone to the prom, like a flash mob serenade. When caught on social media, the expectations heighten – to be spectacular and to receive a "Yes." A "No" becomes a public humiliation.

3. Outline the most important points but leave blanks for the crucial concepts

Example of self-test:

A "prom-posal" is _____
Social media heightens expectations to:
    1. _____
    2. _____
A "No" response could cause _____

4. **Fill** in the blanks without looking at the text.
5. Look at the text, check and correct your responses.

Mnemonics
Mnemonics systems are special techniques to help memorization.
    Examples:
- The acronym *HOMES* to remember the Great Lakes:
  Huron, **O**ntario, **M**ichigan, **E**rie, **S**uperior.
- The sentence for the planets: *My Very Eager Mother Just Served Us Nothing* –
  Mercury, **V**enus, **E**arth, **M**ars, **J**upiter, **S**aturn, **U**ranus, **N**eptune
- Clues within words for plant reproductive organs –
  sta**men** *(male)* and stig**ma** *(female "ma")*.
- Stala**g**tite (**G**) Ground – Stala**c**mite (**C**) Ceiling

Have Fun
Use mnemonics or create your own method to boost your brain's memory power.

I will remember _____ with this technique:

_____
_____
_____

TEENS – ACTIONS, CONSEQUENCES, REWARDS

Academics

FOR THE FACILITATOR

I. Purpose
To reduce scholastic stress, reinforce time spent on homework, and use active study techniques.

II. Skills
Plot own level of stress on a ten point scale in seven scholastic achievement categories.
Identify six or more positive reinforcers and use them as homework rewards.
Gradually increase time on task and attention span.
Practice a self-quiz technique to improve focus and retention.
Demonstrate mnemonics to memorize facts.
State at least two academic consequences of sleep deprivation and two rewards of adequate sleep.

III. Possible Activities
Distribute the *Academics* handouts one at a time and as suggested below:

Academics – Stress Graph
a. Distribute the handout; a volunteer reads the directions, column headings, and example aloud.
b. Allow time for completion.
c. Encourage teens to share their responses and receive peer feedback.

   Possibilities for the "How to handle each issue" entries
   - Pressure about grades – share stress with parents/caregivers; do one's best within reason.
   - Pressure at home and/or work – ask for help from teachers, tutors, etc., and talk with counselor.
   - Fear of being disliked – if due to high grades, don't brag and do offer to help peers; if due to low grades, join a study group, find a study partner; remember that test scores are people's private business.
   - Snowed under – build up confidence with an easy task first.
   - Never enough time – prioritize one's life; delete unproductive activities but do allow some fun!
   - Difficulty being organized – use a daily planner and keep everything on one calendar.
   - Problems focusing on the work – set aside a time and place for homework with no distractions.

Academics – Timely Rewards
   - Start with a *Rewards Bee* in which teens stand and take turns stating positive reinforcers; teens who cannot name a new reward sit down. Continue for a few go rounds or until no one is standing.
   - Distribute the handout. Ask teens to practice each time interval for two days and tell the group how the system is working. Have a class party or other reward when teens spend sixty or more minutes on task.

Academics – Techniques
   - Distribute the page; volunteers read the instructions and examples aloud.
   - *Quiz Yourself* – Teens fill in the blanks and correct their own quizzes.
   - Encourage teens to try the technique to prepare for their next test.
   - Mnemonics – expect a variety of individual responses.
   - Suggest that teens create flash cards or develop test questions for themselves or a study group.

IV. Enrichment Activities
a. Encourage a discussion about the importance of adequate sleep and its effect on academics.
   Possibilities
   - Consequences of sleep deprivation – fall asleep in class, poor concentration, irritability.
   - Rewards of adequate sleep – improved alertness, concentration, memory, mood and health.
b. Ask about ways to improve sleep (set a bedtime and stick to it; no talking or texting after a specified time; adopt a relaxation routine before bed – meditation, progressive muscle relaxation, etc.).

Circumstances

You Can Help No Matter What!

People sometimes find themselves in situations in which their skills do not match exactly what is needed at the moment. However, everyone can help in some way, no matter what.

Each scenario has more than one positive response. Place a check mark in the boxes in front of all positive reactions. You may add your own positive response.

Phone Number Predicament
    You are on a committee planning a festival.
    People exchange phone numbers.
    No one asks for yours.
                   You …
                   ☐ Ask for their phone numbers.
                   ☐ Quit after the first meeting.
                   ☐ Offer your phone number.
                   ☐ Tell the advisor that people are ignoring you.
                   ☐ Other _____

Committee Predicament
    The committee wants people to sign up for one of the following:
        Paint faces of young children who attend.
        Play an instrument to entertain attendees.
        Manage sound equipment.
        Make decorations.
        You feel you lack skills in all areas.
                   You …
                   ☐ Offer to set up and clean up.
                   ☐ Admit you are inexperienced but willing to learn.
                   ☐ Offer your writing skills to advertise the event.
                   ☐ Decide you're not needed and drop out.
                   ☐ Other _____

My Predicament
Write your own scenario anonymously below with some positive and at least one negative option. Then cut or tear your scenario on the broken line.

✂--

Scenario _____

_____

_____

You …
☐ _____

☐ _____

☐ _____

☐ _____

☐ Other _____

TEENS – ACTIONS, CONSEQUENCES, REWARDS

You Can Help No Matter What!

FOR THE FACILITATOR

I. Purpose
To find ways to fit into appropriate settings and determine when to opt out.

II. Skills
Discriminate between two positive and two negative ways to handle exclusion.
Identify three positive ways to fit in and an avoiding action in a scenario about feeling inadequate.
Describe a predicament with four options for peers to contemplate.
Point out positive and negative results from among four options for each peer-created scenario.
Name at least four situations in which it is advisable to opt out rather than try to fit in.

III. Possible Activities
   a. Ask teens to share a predicament in which they wanted to help but felt they lacked the needed skills.
   b. Explain that teens will participate in a preliminary practice and then create scenarios for a game.
   c. Distribute the *You Can Help No Matter What!* handout. A volunteer reads the directions aloud.
   d. Allow time for completion.
   e. Encourage teens to share responses and receive peer feedback.
   Possibilities
   - *Phone Number Predicament* – the first and third options are positive, plus appropriate "Other" responses.
   - *Committee Predicament* – the first three options are positive, plus appropriate "Other" responses.
   f. Review the *My Predicament* guidelines.
   g. Teens will create scenarios and cut or tear on the broken line.
   h. A volunteer collects the scenarios and places them face down at the front of the room.
   The Game Play:
   - Players take turns reading the scenarios and options aloud.
   - Peers point out the positive and negative options.
   - Peers discuss "Other" positive options.

IV. Enrichment Activities
Ask teens to brainstorm situations in which one would NOT want to help.
   Possibilities
   - A peer in trouble with the law asks one to provide an untrue alibi.
   - Clique members expect one to exclude people due to race, ethnicity, sexual orientation, etc.
   - Acquaintances ask one to obtain drugs and alcohol for a party.
   - Students from the next class want one to reveal test questions and answers.
   - Team members want one to join in as they blame one player for the loss of a game.

REWARDS 7

The end is not the reward; the path you take, the emotions that course through you as you grasp life — that is the reward.
~ Jamie Magee

Hope .... page 111 ▶
Teens analyze Emily Dickenson's poem "Hope is the Thing with Feathers" and create a metaphor or other representation of their hope. Teens state when they most need hope and identify its rewards.

Mistakes .... page 113 ▶
Teens personalize quotations about mistakes and discuss decisions to avoid repetition, guilt, denial and shattered self-esteem. Teens state ways mistakes can become valuable learning experiences.

Life is... .... page 115 ▶
Teens identify life's rewards and ways to face its challenges with positivity. Teens incorporate Mother Teresa's ideas and share ways they will implement the suggestions they consider most relevant.

The Glory of Love .... page 117 ▶
Teens personalize concepts from the song's lyrics. Teens share thoughts about love, loss, and what it means when someone sings "a song only you can hear."

REMINDER:
Save completed handouts in "My Actions Book" (see pages 11-14)

Chapter 7 - Rewards Behavioral Coping Skills

Throughout the chapter, teens will communicate through oral, written and creative expression and give and receive feedback.

Teens: Skills in each activity.
Facilitators: Competencies to evaluate.

Hope
- Read a poem and discuss eight or more of its concepts.
- Depict and/or describe hope.
- Complete the sentence "I need my hope most when …"
- Identify five or more rewards of hope.
- Research cultural symbols of hope and create pictorial representations.

Mistakes
- Read a quote and discuss that after the first time a mistake is a decision.
- List the rewards of the decision to NOT repeat the mistake.
- Describe a positive risk that entails mistakes that are not deadly or dangerous.
- State the willingness to learn from mistakes enroute to the goal.
- Identify and elaborate about four or more unproductive ways to handle mistakes.
- Research mistake-related quotations for ten minutes and apply wisdom to own life.
- Personalize interpretations of three inspirational quotations about the rewards of mistakes.
- Compose own words of wisdom about the value of mistakes.

Life is …
- Complete fourteen life-related sentence starters with own ideas.
- Note how Mother Teresa completed the statements.
- Discuss own, peers' and Mother Teresa's ideas about the aspects of life.
- Identify three or more of life's rewards as perceived by Mother Teresa and/or self.
- Personalize the most meaningful Mother Teresa idea – state ways to implement it and its benefits.

The Glory of Love
- Read song lyrics and apply them to a significant platonic, familial or romantic relationship.
- State one or more intangible item given to and taken from a relationship.
- Acknowledge one or more heartbreaking issue that is ongoing or could occur.
- Share about the story and glory of love.
- Identify three or more positive outcomes of lost love.

Rewards

Hope

Hope is the Thing with Feathers
By Emily Dickinson

"Hope" is the thing with feathers
That perches in the soul,
And sings the tune without the words,
And never stops at all,

And sweetest in the gale is heard;
And sore must be the storm
That could abash the little bird
That kept so many warm.

I've heard it in the chillest land
And on the strangest sea;
Yet, never, in extremity,
It asked a crumb from me.

Use sketches, symbols, and/or words to describe your hope.

My hope …

I need my hope most when …

TEENS – ACTIONS, CONSEQUENCES, REWARDS

Hope

FOR THE FACILITATOR

I. Purpose
To analyze a poet's concept of hope, create a metaphor or other visual or verbal representation of one's hope and determine its benefits.

II. Skills
Read Emily Dickinson's poem about hope.
Discuss eight or more of the poem's concepts.
Create a metaphor or other representation of hope.
State when hope is most needed.
Identify five or more rewards of hope.

III. Possible Activities
    a. Write "Hope" on the board; ask teens what comes to mind (expect various personalized responses).
    b. Distribute the *Hope* handout; a volunteer reads the poem and directions aloud.
    c. Ask teens for their spins on the lines.
    d. Emphasize that there are no wrong responses; poetry is open to individual interpretation.
    Some possible interpretations
    The extended metaphor compares hope to a bird. In the poem, hope …
- Symbolizes courage and confidence to soar above problems
- Has feathers that warm and protect
- Can be felt without words as a desire or expectation
- Is at its best during a "sore" or severe crisis
- Safeguards one from feeling "abashed" or deflated and humiliated
- Comforts in the "chillest land" or an unfriendly and uncaring circumstance
- Helps in the "strangest sea" or an unfamiliar and scary situation
- Never asks "a crumb" or can be effortless if one believes

    e. Remind teens that artistic ability, perfect grammar or spelling are not needed for this activity.
    f. Ask teens to draw, symbolize, write poetry or prose, etc., to represent what "hope" means to them.
    g. Expect a variety of personal responses.
    Possibilities for *My hope …*

Angel	Rainbow
Blossom	Religious symbol or entity
Butterfly	Star or the sun
Bridge	The little engine that could

    Possibilities for *I need my hope most when …*
    People fight at home
    I feel rejected
    I think I can't

IV. Enrichment Activities
    a. Ask teens to brainstorm the rewards of maintaining hope.
    Examples – a person who has hope will persevere toward a goal, survive set-backs, inspire others, find possibilities in problems, believe the best about people, etc.
    b. Suggest teens research cultural symbols of hope (dove, dream catcher) and create posters.
    c. Encourage artistic teens to illustrate the poem.

Rewards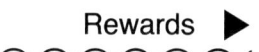

Mistakes

It is valuable to learn from our mistakes!

> When you repeat a mistake, it is not a mistake any more: it's a decision.
> ~ Paulo Coelho

A mistake I once repeated was _____

_____

The consequences were _____

_____

A mistake I am tempted to repeat is _____

_____

The consequences could be _____

_____

If I make the decision NOT to repeat the same mistake, my rewards will be _____

_____

Sometimes mistakes lead to success!

Think about something new and great you'd like to try.

The goal may involve mistakes – be sure they are not deadly or dangerous!

Remember – Thomas Edison "found ten thousand ways it won't work" when inventing the light bulb.

What passion will you pursue?

How will your mistakes become rewards?

Mistakes

FOR THE FACILITATOR

I. **Purpose**
   To recognize that to repeat a mistake is a decision; to decide in favor of one's safety and welfare; to decide to take a positive risk, and to learn from non-life-threatening mistakes.

II. **Skills**
   Read a quotation and discuss that repeating a mistake is a decision.
   Identify a repeated mistake and the consequences.
   List the rewards of the decision to not repeat the mistake.
   Describe a positive risk that entails potential mistakes that are not deadly or dangerous.
   State the willingness to learn from mistakes made en route to the goal.
   Identify and elaborate about at least four unproductive ways to handle mistakes.
   Research mistake-related quotations for ten minutes and apply their wisdom to own life.
   Personalize interpretation of three inspirational quotations about the rewards of mistakes.
   Compose own words of wisdom about the value of mistakes.

III. **Possible Activities**
   a. Ask for a show of hands from people who have played video games that test speed and skill.
   b. Pose the question "How do you get better at the games?" (Practice; avoid previous mistakes).
   c. Encourage a brief discussion about mistakes made in video games and what was learned.
   d. Tell teens they will consider mistakes they made or could make that are more serious than in games.
   e. Distribute the *Mistakes* handout; a volunteer reads the quotation aloud.
   f. Assure teens that their responses are private unless they choose to share.
   g. Allow time for completion.
   h. Encourage teens to share their responses and receive peer feedback.
      Responses will be individual except the last question in the bottom section:
      How will your mistakes become rewards?
      Elicit that mistakes can be valuable learning experiences.
   i. Ask teens to brainstorm unproductive ways to handle mistakes; a volunteer lists ideas on the board.
      Possibilities
      - Guilt – to blame oneself is depressing; decide to change and then follow through.
      - Denial – to lie to others or oneself avoids the issue; face it and move forward.
      - Panic – to over-react leads to stress and clouded thinking; analyze the causes and solutions.
      - Shattered self-esteem – to examine one's mistakes takes confidence; learn and gain wisdom.

IV. **Enrichment Activities**
   a. Initiate a *Mistakes Quotes Fest*.
      - Individuals or teams research as many quotes about mistakes as possible in ten minutes.
      - Teens share their findings and give their own real life examples of each.
   b. After teens share their findings, write the following quotations on the board and encourage teens to personalize the messages:
      The only true mistake is the one from which we learn nothing. ~ John Powell
      You make mistakes. Mistakes don't make you. ~ Maxwell Maltz
      Creativity is allowing yourself to make mistakes. Art is knowing which ones to keep. ~ Scott Adams
      The secret of life… is to fall seven times and to get up eight times. ~ Paulo Coelho
   c. Ask teens to compose their own words of wisdom about mistakes, then share and receive feedback.

Life is...

Before you start, please fold the bottom of the page under on the broken line.
Complete the ideas with your own words.
Example – Life is an opportunity, benefit from it.

1. Life is an opportunity, _____
2. Life is beauty, _____
3. Life is a dream, _____
4. Life is a challenge, _____
5. Life is a duty, _____
6. Life is a game, _____
7. Life is a promise, _____
8. Life is sorrow, _____
9. Life is a song, _____
10. Life is a struggle, _____
11. Life is a tragedy, _____
12. Life is an adventure, _____
13. Life is luck, _____
14. Life is life, _____

FOLD THE BOTTOM OF THIS PAGE UNDER ON THE BROKEN LINE

**Guess how Mother Teresa* completed the sentences.
Many of her words can apply to more than one.**

Sentence completions in random order

confront it   sing it   fulfill it   complete it   realize it   benefit from it   accept it

fight for it   overcome it   play it   meet it   make it   admire it   dare it

*Mother Teresa was a religious sister and missionary, admired for her charitable works. The sentences are excerpts from her poem LIFE which can be viewed in its entirety on the Internet.

TEENS – ACTIONS, CONSEQUENCES, REWARDS

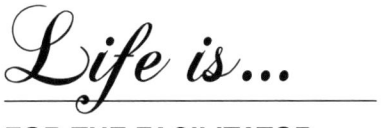

Life is...

FOR THE FACILITATOR

I. **Purpose**
   To identify life's rewards and face its challenges with positivity.

II. **Skills**
   Complete fourteen life-related sentence starters with own ideas.
   Note how Mother Teresa completed the sentences.
   Discuss own ideas and/or those generated by self, peers and Mother Teresa regarding the addressed aspects of life.
   State at least one positive way to face a sorrow, struggle or tragedy based on the sentence completions.
   Identify at least three of life's rewards as perceived by Mother Teresa and/or self.
   Personalize the most meaningful Mother Teresa idea – state ways to implement it and the benefits.

III. **Possible Activities**
   a. Ask teens to share their feelings about people who interrupt to finish their sentences during conversations. (Possibly annoyed by people who assume they know what will be said; possibly okay with a friend who knows them well enough to predict).
   b. Tell teens they will finish some sentences and later guess a Nobel Peace Prize winner's completions.
   c. Distribute the *Life Is ...* handout; a volunteer reads the directions aloud.
   d. Direct teens to fold under the bottom of the page on the broken line.
   e. Prompt teens to use their imaginations when they finish the sentence starters.
   f. Encourage teens to share their responses and receive peer feedback.
   g. Ask teens to unfold the bottoms of their papers.
   h. Suggest that teens take turns reading the sentence starters aloud and calling out the completions they think Mother Teresa composed; they are listed in random order in the box at the bottom of the page.
   i. Advise teens that there are no wrong responses; some starters have more than one possible response.
   Mother Teresa's completions:

1. Benefit from it	5. Complete it	9. Sing it	13. Make it
2. Admire it	6. Play it	10. Accept it	14. Fight for it
3. Realize it	7. Fulfill it	11. Confront it	
4. Meet it	8. Overcome it	12. Dare it	

   j. Reinforce Mother Teresa's ways to handle hardships (overcome, accept, confront).
   k. Ask teens how these suggestions help them face a current sorrow, struggle or tragedy.
   l. Encourage teens to share their impressions of Mother Teresa's ideas about other positive aspects of life.
   m. Pose the question: "What are life's rewards as you see them or as suggested by Mother Teresa?" Expect a variety of personalized responses plus other possible interpretations – life is beauty, a dream, a promise, an adventure; you make your own luck, sing your own song, fight for the best.

IV. **Enrichment Activities**
   Ask teens to write on the back of their papers and/or share aloud their ideas about the following:
   • Which of Mother Teresa's suggestions is most meaningful to each teen and why
   • Ways teens will implement the suggestion
   • Ways teens will benefit
   Responses will be personal.

The Glory of Love

"You've got to give a little, take a little,
And let your poor heart break a little.
That's the story of, that's the glory of love."
By Billy Hill

I give …

_____

I take …

_____

My heart breaks …

_____

_____

The story of my love …

_____

_____

The glory of my love …

_____

_____

If you love, you will at some point experience the pain of loss
- a break up, an ended friendship, a death.

Alfred Lord Tennyson said … *Better to have loved and lost than never to have loved at all.*

Explain what the above quotation means to you.

_____

_____

_____

The Glory of Love

FOR THE FACILITATOR

I. Purpose
To identify the rewards of love and loss.

II. Skills
Read the song lyrics of *The Glory of Love* by Billy Hill and apply them to own friendships, familial or romantic relationships.
State one or more intangible item that people give and take from a relationship.
Acknowledge one or more heartbreaking issue that is ongoing or could occur.
Share ideas about the *story* and *glory* of love.
Describe three or more characteristics of unconditional love.
Identify three or more positive outcomes of lost love.

III. Possible Activities
a. If possible find a recording, or the music and lyrics on the internet, and encourage teens to sing along.
b. Encourage a discussion about the different types of love (familial, friendship, romantic, etc.).
c. Distribute *The Glory of Love* handout. A volunteer reads the excerpt aloud.
d. Allow time for completion.
e. Encourage teens to share their responses and receive peer feedback.
   Possibilities
   I give … love, time, energy, respect, my deepest thoughts, my most private feelings, etc.
   I take … love, time, energy, the person's opinions and feelings to heart, constructive criticism, etc.
   My heart breaks … at the thought of loss, when we disagree, when my loved one is in pain, etc.
   The story of my love … (individualized responses).
   The glory of my love … (individualized responses).
f. Ask teens to brainstorm aspects of unconditional love. A volunteer lists ideas on the board.
   Possibilities
   • Mutuality
   • Forgiveness
   • Acceptance of oneself and the other person, not trying to change the person
   • Discovery of one's own and the other person's worth and attributes
   • Completeness; not needing the other person to feel whole
g. Regarding the question about the Tennyson quotation, *Explain what this means to you.* Responses will be individual. Encourage a discussion.

IV. Enrichment Activities
a. Write the following quotation on the board:
   "You don't love someone for their looks, or their clothes, or for their fancy car, but because they sing a song only you can hear." ~ Oscar Wilde
b. Encourage teens to interpret and personalize the words.
   Possibilities
   The *song* that is mutually heard may be each other's feelings, common interests, similar pasts; the chemistry between them; their senses of humor, life views, faith, etc.

RECAP OF ACTIONS, CONSEQUENCES, REWARDS

Memory is a way of holding onto the things you love, the things you are, the things you never want to lose.

~ The Wonder Years

Reward Extraordinaire .... page **121** ▶
Teens review and self-assess their understanding of concepts presented in earlier sessions and describe their current and future rewards. Teens identify the most valuable concepts they learned about themselves in each of the chapters.

Recap – My Actions Book .... page **125** ▶
Teens compile and/or complete notebooks incorporating pages created during prior sessions, plus ideas related to soundtracks, favorites, pictures and additional enhancements.

Recap Behavioral Coping Skills

Throughout the chapter, teens will communicate through oral, written and creative expression and give and receive feedback.

Teens: Skills in each activity.
Facilitators: Competencies to evaluate.

Reward Extraordinaire
- Complete thirty eight items – matching, fill in the blanks, multiple choice, true-false, etc.
- Write current rewards and rewards being worked on.
- Identify the most valuable self-concept learned in each of the chapters.

Recap – *My Actions Book*
- Organize accomplishments by creating a special notebook.
- Apply musical lyrics to past, present and future by selecting relevant songs.
- Describe how music, literature, theater, media and art apply to actions, consequences and rewards.
- Describe the most meaningful activity, most important concept and how to apply it to life.
- Reflect on a quotation, look through *My Actions Book*, and identify rewards.

Recap

Reward Extraordinaire

Healthy & Unhealthy Risks – Write the matching letter next to its numbered statement.
1. _____ Injury or damage may occur
2. _____ Reckless driving
3. _____ Monitors environmental cues
4. _____ Answer a question in class
5. _____ Helps determine success or failure

a. Mind-set
b. Example of an unhealthy risk
c. Example of a positive risk
d. Definition of an unhealthy risk
e. An early warning system

Decisions – Circle the letter in front of the best response.
1. To promote a positive outcome
   a. Impulsively rush in.
   b. Stop and think.
2. Denial of a problem.
   a. Delays solving it.
   b. Makes it go away.
3. When making decisions
   a. Always let your head rule your heart.
   b. Both thoughts and feelings are important.
4. In a moment of extreme danger when you must act quickly
   a. Consider your fight or flight instincts.
   b. Ignore your fight or flight response.

Types of Consequences and Rewards - Write "T" if it is true or "F" false.
1. _____ All consequences are imposed by the legal system.
2. _____ An internal consequence or reward is thought or felt privately.
3. _____ A person who sticks up for someone who is mistreated experiences an internal reward.

Dangers – Circle the letter in front of the best response.
1. Addiction is
   a. Based on genetics, biology and dopamine levels exclusively.
   b. Related to biological and environmental factors.
2. Recovery is
   a. A one time quick fix.
   b. A process that takes time and effort.
3. Campus violence
   a. Requires everyone to be alert.
   b. Would never happen here.
4. Eating disorders
   a. Are treated by strict diet and strenuous exercise.
   b. Are related to physical and emotional issues.
5. A car is a great place for
   a. A party, joking, drinking and speeding.
   b. Focus, seat belts, following rules.
6. When it comes to sex
   a. Everybody is doing it.
   b. Not everybody is doing it.
7. People who cut on themselves
   a. Usually have painful emotions.
   b. Do it for fun.
8. Finish this Japanese proverb –
   Fall seven times
   a. Stay down the seventh time.
   b. Stand up eight.
9. When in a gang
   a. Once a member, always a member.
   b. Interventionists and others can help people leave.
10. If a friend is handling a gun
    a. Leave and tell a trusted adult.
    b. Stay and get a closer look.
11. Jealousy
    a. Proves that one partner loves the other.
    b. Suggests that a partner is insecure.
12. Regarding bullying
    a. It is totally the fault of the person who bullies.
    b. Bystanders have a responsibility.

(Continued on the next page)

TEENS – ACTIONS, CONSEQUENCES, REWARDS

Reward Extraordinaire (Continued)

Attributes – Fill in the blanks from the word bank.

> **Word Bank:**   optimism   peaceful   transparency   health

1. Nutrition, exercise and sleep promote _____.
2. An example of a positive trait is _____.
3. "What you see is what you get" is an example of _____.
4. Instead of violent rebellion – do research, gather support and work for _____ change.

Circumstances –Write "T" if the statement is true and "F" if it is false.

1. _____ People who grow up in families with dysfunction are doomed forever.
2. _____ People who seem different are usually more similar to us then we realize.
3. _____ It is usually easier to prevent a problem than to solve it.
4. _____ One person cannot do much to change the world.
5. _____ Study three hours straight with no breaks.
6. _____ One must fit in everywhere all of the time.

Rewards – Circle the letter in front of the best response.

1. Hope is
    a. A pie in the sky fantasy.
    b. A life sustaining force.
2. When a mistake is repeated it is
    a. A decision.
    b. An accident.
3. Life can be
    a. Scary – run from it.
    b. Exciting – embrace it.
4. Love involves
    a. Pleasure and pain.
    b. Continuous joy.

Recap - Looking back at my work, the most valuable concepts I learned about myself …

My risks _____

My decisions _____

My consequences _____

My rewards _____

My dangers _____

My attributes _____

My circumstances _____

My most valuable reward _____

Reward Celebration

Write your rewards on the scrolls.

I am thankful for these rewards ...

I work toward these rewards ...

TEENS – ACTIONS, CONSEQUENCES, REWARDS

Reward Extraordinaire
FOR THE FACILITATOR

I. Purpose
To review many of the concepts presented in previous sessions.

II. Skills
Match five definitions and examples related to healthy and unhealthy risks.
Select four correct sentence completions regarding decisions.
Identify three statements as true or false regarding types of consequences and rewards.
Choose the best completions for twelve sentences related to dangers.
Place four terms in the correct blanks regarding possibilities.
Label six statements as true or false related to circumstances.
Indicate the best completions for four sentence stems related to rewards.
Describe current rewards and anticipated future rewards.
Identify the most valuable concept learned in each chapter.

III. Possible Activities
a. Explain that teens will complete a review activity; state it is not a test and it will be self-scored.
b. Distribute the *Reward Extraordinaire* handout – two review pages and one journaling page.
c. Allow time for completion; review responses as a group.

Answer Key

Healthy and Unhealthy Risks
  1.d 2.b 3.e 4.c 5.a

Decisions
  1.b 2.a 3.b 4.a

Types of Rewards and Consequences
  1.F 2.T 3.T

Dangers
  1.b 2.b 3.a 4.b 5.b 6.b 7.a 8.b 9.b 10.a 11.b 12.b

Attributes
  health   optimism   transparency   peaceful

Circumstances
  1.F 2.T 3.T 4.F 5.F 6.F

Rewards
  1.b 2.a 3.b 4.a

Recap
  Responses will be individual. Encourage teens to share responses and receive peer feedback.

Rewards Celebration
  Responses will be individual. Encourage teens to share responses and receive peer feedback.

IV. Enrichment Activity
If teens have saved their handouts as suggested in this book's *Introduction*, encourage them to share about their most meaningful pages.

Recap – *My Actions Book*

1. **If you have not already created *My Actions Book* take time now to organize.**

    - Place the your completed activity handouts in a three ring binder or affix into a scrapbook or notebook.
    - Name your book and give it a subtitle.
    - Add pertinent articles, website information, poems, etc.
    - Create a *Table of Contents*.
    - For each chapter, create a cover page with a quote written by you or someone else.
    - Decorate the cover.

2. **If you already created your book, or when it is all organized – add to it.**

    - Add page(s) titled *The Soundtrack of My Life*.

        Attach lyrics that relate to your past and present life.

    - Add page(s) titled *My Future Soundtrack*

        Attach lyrics that relate to your future hopes, dreams and goals.

    - Add page(s) titled *My Favorites*

        List books, poems, movies, plays, television shows, videos, websites, etc.

    - Add page(s) titled *My Picture Gallery*.

        Attach photos, art, cartoons, etc.

3. **On each page, describe how each entry applies to your actions, consequences and rewards.**

Recap – *My Actions Book*

Regarding *Teens ~ Actions, Consequences, Rewards*

As you review your activities, respond to the following sentence starters.

My most meaningful activity was …

What really sticks with me is …

I will apply this concept to my life by …

Recap – *My Actions Book*

Rewards of a Thing Well Done

> *The reward of a thing well done is having done it.*
> ~ Ralph Waldo Emerson

Looking back through your "My Actions Book" – what have been your rewards?

_____
_____
_____
_____
_____
_____
_____
_____
_____
_____
_____
_____
_____
_____
_____
_____
_____
_____
_____

TEENS – ACTIONS, CONSEQUENCES, REWARDS

Recap – *My Actions Book*

FOR THE FACILITATOR

I. Purpose
To preserve memories and insights acquired during the book's activities.
To augment these through the written word, music, media and art.

II. Skills
Organize accomplishments by creating a special notebook.
Apply musical lyrics to the past, present, and future by selecting relevant songs.
Describe how music, literature, theater, media, and art apply to actions, consequences, and rewards.
Describe the most meaningful activity, most important concept, and how to apply it to life.

III. Possible Activities
a. The day before the Recap activity remind teens to bring *My Actions Book* notebook or scrapbook to the session, or have these available for teens.
b. Distribute the Recap – *My Actions Book* handout, page 125.
c. Allow time for completion.
d. Distribute *Regarding the Actions, Consequences, Rewards* handout page 126.
e. Allow time for completion.
f. Distribute *Rewards of a Thing Well Done* handout, page 127.
g. Allow time for completion.
h. Encourage teens to share their soundtracks, favorites and responses and receive peer feedback.

IV. Enrichment Activity
Encourage teens to consider their notebooks a work-in-progress and keep them to add future handouts, articles, journal entries, art work, lyrics, and favorites that relate to actions, consequences, and rewards.

wholeperson

Whole Person Associates is the leading publisher of training resources for professionals who empower people to create and maintain healthy lifestyles. Our creative resources will help you work effectively with your clients in the areas of stress management, wellness promotion, mental health and life skills.

Please visit us at our web site: **www.wholeperson.com**. You can check out our entire line of products, place an order, request our print catalog, and sign up for our monthly special notifications.

Whole Person Associates
800-247-6789